The United States and Europe in the Twentieth Century

D0293538

For Daniel Norman Ryan, Hannah Storeheier Ryan and Heidi Storeheier

SEMINAR STUDIES   IN HISTORY

The United States and Europe in the Twentieth Century

DAVID RYAN

PEARSON

Longman

London • New York • Toronto • Sydney • Tokyo • Singapore
Hong Kong • Cape Town • Madrid • Paris • Amsterdam • Munich • Milan

PEARSON EDUCATION LIMITED

Head Office:
Edinburgh Gate
Harlow CM20 2JE
Tel: +44 (0)1279 623623
Fax: +44 (0)1279 431059

London Office:
128 Long Acre
London WC2E 9AN
Tel: +44 (0)20 7447 2000
Fax: +44 (0)20 7447 2170
Website: www.history-minds.com

First published in Great Britain in 2003

© Pearson Education Limited 2003

The right of David Ryan to be identified as Author
of this Work has been asserted by him in accordance
with the Copyright, Designs and Patents Act 1988.

ISBN 0 582 30864 X
British Library Cataloguing in Publication Data
A CIP catalogue record for this book can be obtained from the British Library

Library of Congress Cataloging in Publication Data
A CIP catalog record for this book can be obtained from the Library of Congress

All rights reserved; no part of this publication may be reproduced, stored
in a retrieval system, or transmitted in any form or by any means, electronic,
mechanical, photocopying, recording, or otherwise without either the prior
written permission of the Publishers or a licence permitting restricted copying
in the United Kingdom issued by the Copyright Licensing Agency Ltd,
90 Tottenham Court Road, London, W1T 4LP. This book may not be lent,
resold, hired out or otherwise disposed of by way of trade in any form
of binding or cover other than that in which it is published, without the
prior consent of the Publishers.

Transferred to digital print on demand, 2006

Typeset by 7 in 10/12 Sabon Roman
Produced by Pearson Education Asia Pte Ltd.,

Printed and bound by CPI Antony Rowe, Eastbourne

CONTENTS

INTRODUCTION TO THE SERIES

Such is the pace of historical enquiry in the modern world that there is an ever-widening gap between the specialist article or monograph, incorporating the results of current research, and general surveys, which inevitably become out of date. *Seminar Studies in History* is designed to bridge this gap. The series was founded by Patrick Richardson in 1966 and his aim was to cover major themes in British, European and world history. Between 1980 and 1996 Roger Lockyer continued his work, before handing the editorship over to Clive Emsley and Gordon Martel. Clive Emsley is Professor of History at the Open University, while Gordon Martel is Professor of International History at the University of Northern British Columbia, Canada, and Senior Research Fellow at De Montfort University.

All the books are written by experts in their field who are not only familiar with the latest research but have often contributed to it. They are frequently revised, in order to take account of new information and interpretations. They provide a selection of documents to illustrate major themes and provoke discussion, and also a guide to further reading. The aim of *Seminar Studies in History* is to clarify complex issues without over-simplifying them, and to stimulate readers into deepening their knowledge and understanding of major themes and topics.

AUTHOR'S ACKNOWLEDGEMENTS

In a study of such length one is bound to sometimes deal in generalities. In this book the word 'Europe' has often been used to describe essential positions which the United States either worried about or attributed as though the continent was unified. Of course the continent has not been unified throughout the twentieth century and there were always exceptional positions even within the various unions. Word space has not permitted an analysis of all the individual responses. I alone am responsible for any errors in fact or interpretation. Special thanks are due to Gordon Martel who encouraged me to work on this project and who provided guidance, editorial advice and general support throughout. Thanks are also due to Maurice Fitzgerald for his encouragement and discussion and for opportunities to discuss sections at his European Studies seminar and to Mark Bell for similar encouragement. Thanks are due to Ian Jackson for providing stimulating conversation and insight into US policy over the years. De Montfort University provided time to complete the project, for which I am grateful. Especial gratitude is also due to Heidi Storeheier for her support and patience throughout, and to Daniel and Hannah. Thanks are also due to Casey Mein, Hilary Shaw, Yvonne Blow and Magda Robson.

PUBLISHER'S ACKNOWLEDGEMENTS

We are grateful to NATO for permission to reproduce extracts from their online library at www.nato.int.

LIST OF MAPS

CHRONOLOGY

1897– 1901

William McKinley administration; Secretaries of State: John Sherman 1897–98; William Day, 1898; John Hay 1898–1905.

1898

11 April
US goes to war with Spain over Cuba and the Philippines.

1901–09

Theodore Roosevelt administration; Secretaries of State: John Hay 1898–1905; Elihu Root 1905–09; Robert Bacon 1909.

1909–13

William Howard Taft administration; Secretary of State: Philander Knox.

1913–21

Woodrow Wilson administration; Secretaries of State: William Jennings Bryan 1913–15; Robert Lansing 1915–20; Bainbridge Colby 1920–21.

1914

28 June
Assassination of Archduke Franz Ferdinand in Sarajevo. First World War begins and intensifies after the German declaration of war on Russia on 1 August.

2 November
British blockade of Germany begins; North Sea declared a war zone.

1915

7 May
Lusitania sunk by German U-boats off the southern Irish coast. US protests against the action, but does not enter the war.

1916

12 December
Central Powers make a peace offer which the Allies reject on 30 December.

1917

31 January	Unrestricted submarine warfare resumed by Germany.
12 March	Russian revolution leads to Tsar Nicholas II's abdication. Duma replaces Tsarist government.
6 April	US declares war on Germany; US troops arrive in Europe in June.
18 May	Kerensky leads provisional government in Russia.
8 September	Kornilov affair exposed by Kerensky in Russia.
7 November	Bolshevik Revolution in Russia; Lenin assumes power. The following day Lenin forms a government and calls for a peace.
7 December	US enters war against Austro-Hungarian Empire.
17 December	Russia and Germany agree on a cease-fire at Brest-Litovsk.

1918

8 January	President Woodrow Wilson announces the Fourteen Points as the basis on which to bring the war to an end.
3 March	Brest-Litovsk: Bolsheviks accept the terms of peace offered by Germany.
23 June	Allied forces arrive in Murmansk, Russia.
14 August	US forces arrive in Vladiviostok, Russia.
3 October	Germany seeks to negotiate surrender based on the Fourteen Points.
23 October	Wilson refuses to negotiate peace terms with the Kaiser, who abdicates in November.
9 November	Germans create a republic.
11 November	Armistice agreed in the West.

1919

15 January	Rosa Luxemburg and Karl Liebknecht killed after revolt in Berlin by the German Communist Party.
28 June	The Treaty of Versailles. League of Nations created. US Senate rejects membership in March 1920.

1921–23

	Warren Harding administration; Secretary of State: Charles Evans Hughes.

1922

6 February	Washington Treaty signed by US, Britain, France, Italy and Japan, which limits the size of their navies.

March	Stalin assumes post of General Secretary. Lenin suffers a stroke in May 1922. Lenin dies 21 January 1924.
30 October	Mussolini arrives in Rome and forms a cabinet the following day. Dictatorial power assumed in November.
30 December	Union of Soviet Socialist Republics (USSR) formed.

1923–29

Calvin Coolidge administration; Secretary of State: Frank Kellogg 1925–29.

1924

9 April	Dawes Plan advanced by US bankers, backed by President Coolidge, which facilitates payment of German reparations to Allied governments and Allied repayments of loans to US.

1925

1 December	Locarno Treaty guarantees borders between France and Germany and between Germany and Belgium.

1928

27 August	Kellogg–Briand Pact signed by US, France and 62 nations, outlawing war and requiring settlement of disputes through negotiation.

1929–33

Herbert Hoover administration; Secretary of State: Henry Stimson 1929–33.

1929

6 February	Germany joins Kellogg–Briand Pact.
7 June	US Young Plan reschedules and reduces German reparation payments.
29 October	Wall Street Crash in New York. US credit for Europeans cease.

1932

31 July	Nazis win 230 seats in *Reichstag* becoming the largest party.

1933–45

Franklin D. Roosevelt administration; Secretary of State: Cordell Hull 1933–44; Edward Stettinius 1944–45.

1933

30 January	Hitler becomes Chancellor in Germany.
November	US recognises Soviet Union.

1934

June	US Reciprocal Trade Act.

1935

31 August	US Neutrality Act passed. Further acts passed in 1936 and 1937.
15 September	Nuremberg Laws passed in Germany.
3 October	Italy invades Ethiopia.

1936

7 March	Germany violates the Versailles Treaty, occupying the Rhineland.
18 July	Spanish Civil War begins, lead by General Franco. War concludes in April 1939.
19 October	Four-year economic plan announced in Germany in preparation for war.
1 November	Axis between Berlin and Rome announced (formed on 24 October).
18 November	Axis recognises Franco's government in Spain.

1938

12 March	German forces enter Austria in the *Anschluss*.
23 April	German forces move into part of Czechoslovakia, the Sudetenland.
30 September	Munich Agreement between Hitler and British Prime Minister Chamberlain gives Sudetenland to Germany, for 'peace in our time'.
9–10 November	*Kristallnacht*: Anti-Jewish violence in Germany.

1939

27 February	Franco's government recognised by Britain and France.
15 March	Germany takes rest of Czechoslovakia.
31 March	Britain and France guarantee Polish sovereignty.
1 April	Spanish Civil War concludes.
23 August	Nazi–Soviet Pact signed by German Foreign Minister Ribbentrop and Soviet Foreign Minister Molotov.
1 September	Germany invades Poland.

3 September	Britain and France declare war on Germany.
30 September	Germany and the Soviet Union divide Poland.
3 November	France and Britain begin 'cash and carry' arrangement with US to obtain arms.

1940

10 May	German attack on Luxembourg, Holland and Belgium. Chamberlain resigns in Britain. Winston Churchill becomes wartime Prime Minister.
12 May	German forces enter France.
29 May	British forces evacuate from Dunkirk, after German advance.
18 June	General de Gaulle organises French government (the Free French) and resistance from London.
June–September	The Battle of Britain.

1941

6 January	President Roosevelt proposes the Lend-Lease Bill to the US Congress, passed in March.
13 April	Soviet Union concludes a non-aggression pact with Japan.
22 June	Nazi Germany invades the Soviet Union in Operation Barbarossa.
14 August	Atlantic Charter signed initially by Roosevelt and Churchill.
7 December	Japanese bomb US fleet at Pearl Harbor.
11 December	Germany and Italy declare war on the United States.

| 1942–43 | Operation Torch begins in North Africa. Anglo-American forces eventually defeat Axis forces in Africa in May 1943. |

1942

| 2 January | Grand Alliance formed between the United States, Britain, the Soviet Union and 23 nations with the common purpose of defeating the Axis powers. |

1943

14–24 January	Roosevelt and Churchill meet at Casablanca to negotiate the German unconditional surrender.
10 July	Allies invade Sicily.
8 September	Italy surrenders; Germany takes over in Italy. Rome falls to the Allies in June 1944.
28 November	Roosevelt, Stalin and Churchill meet for the Tehran Conference.

1944

6 June	Allied forces land in Normandy in Operation Overlord.
1 July	Bretton Woods Conference begins the design of the post-war economic order.
25 August	Paris liberated; de Gaulle's provisional government installed in October.
10 October	Churchill and Stalin conclude the sphere of influence deal allocating power in south-east Europe.

1945–53

Harry Truman administration; Secretaries of State: James Byrnes 1945–1947; George Marshall 1947–1949; Dean Acheson 1949–1953.

1945

4 February	Roosevelt, Churchill and Stalin meet at the Yalta Conference to discuss German surrender and Allied zones of occupation, the Polish settlement and the Declaration for a Liberated Europe.
12 April	Roosevelt dies.
2 May	German surrender to Soviet Union.
7 May	German unconditional surrender in the West.
8 May	VE-Day, Victory in Europe.
17 July– 2 August	Potsdam Conference: Stalin, Truman, Churchill and then Attlee meet to discuss the German occupation and Eastern Europe.

1946

22 February	George Kennan's long telegram sent.
5 March	'Iron Curtain' speech made by Churchill at Fulton, Missouri.

1947

12 March	President Truman's address to the joint session of Congress initiates the Truman Doctrine, requesting aid for Greece and Turkey.
5 June	Marshall plan announced to create the European Recovery Plan (ERP).
12 June	Committee of European Economic Cooperation (CEEC) created to advance plans for European recovery.
July	Mr. X (George Kennan) articulates the US policy of containment.

1948

25 February	Czech coup; Beneš government dominated by communists.
14 March	Congress approves initial Marshall aid.
17 March	Brussels Treaty Organisation on military security set up between Belgium, France, Luxembourg, the Netherlands and Britain.
April	Organisation for European Economic Cooperation created to deal with the Marshall aid.
24 June	Soviets blockade western access to Berlin. The blockade lasts until May 1949. The Berlin airlift re-supplies the city. The Federal Republic of Germany is created as a result. In the East the German Democratic Republic is created in October.
15 August	India and Pakistan granted independence from Britain.

1949

25 June	Soviet and East Europeans create Comecon for economic cooperation.
4 April	North Atlantic Treaty Organisation (NATO) joins the Brussels Treaty Organisation with the United States, Canada, Portugal, Norway, Iceland and Denmark. Collective security is introduced.

1950

14 April	National Security Council Paper 68 (NSC-68), provides a blueprint for US strategy in the Cold War

1951

18 April	Six West European countries set up the European Coal and Steel Community (ECSC). Membership includes France, West Germany, Italy and Luxembourg, the Netherlands and Belgium. Britain refuses to join.

1952

18 February	Greece and Turkey join NATO.
27 May	European Defence Community created to tie in West German power with other West Europeans.

1953–61

	Dwight Eisenhower administration; Secretaries of State: John Foster Dulles 1953–59; Christian Herter 1959–61.

1953

5 March	Stalin dies. Khrushchev and Malenkov vie for power.
June	East German protests are crushed.

1954

May   French forces defeated at Dien Bien Phu resulting in their withdrawal from Indochina.

1955

5 April   Messina Conference proposes a customs union among 'the Six' West European countries

9 May   West Germany enters NATO.

14 May   Warsaw Pact created, joining the states of East Europe with the Soviet Union.

1956

25 February   Khrushchev's secret speech denounces Stalinism and introduces reform.

October   Hungarian revolution begins. By November Soviet intervention suppresses the uprising and deposes the government.

29 October   Israel invades Egypt at Suez; British and French forces follow.

1957

25 March   'The Six' sign the Treaty of Rome creating the European Economic Community (EEC).

1959

20 November   European Free Trade Association (EFTA) set up for greater co-operation in the face of EEC. EFTA, 'the Seven' include Britain, Austria, Norway, Denmark, Sweden, Switzerland and Portugal.

1961–63   John F. Kennedy administration; Secretary of States: Dean Rusk 1961–69.

1961

10 August   Britain, Ireland and Denmark apply to join the EEC. De Gaulle vetoes the British application in January 1963.

17 August   Berlin Wall erected to stem the flow of refugees to the West.

1962

4 July   Kennedy announces Grand Design for Europe, envisaging 'interdependence'.

October   Cuban Missile Crisis between the United States and the Soviet Union; West European allies generally not consulted by Washington.

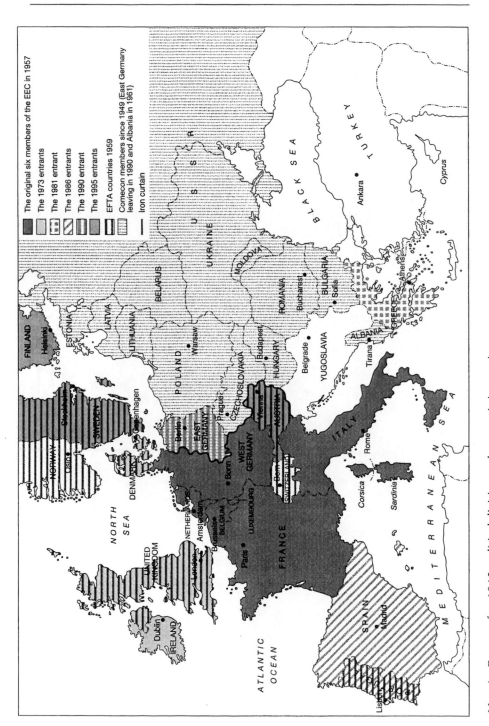

Map 4 Europe after 1945: political division and economic integration
Adapted from O'Brien, P. (1999) *Philip's Atlas of World History* (pub George Philip Ltd.).

PART ONE   BACKGROUND

Mexico in 1846 to conquer over half its territory. The continental empire was finally completed with the Gadsden Purchase (1853), adjusting the borders between the United States and a much-contracted Mexico.

Territorial conquest and border colonisation characterised the process though Americans preferred to term their expansion and the removal of European powers and Native American tribes 'Manifest Destiny'. The term 'border colonisation' refers to an 'extensive opening up of land for human use, pushing a "frontier" into the "wilderness" for agricultural purposes or to attain natural resources' (Osterhammel, 1997: 5). The process required settlement. Agricultural interests, especially the southern tobacco crop, required new lands. Expansion was assisted by an ideology that imputed that 'confinement and inactivity were ... the national nemesis'. Expansion was therefore the answer to the vexed question on the degeneration of republican democracy. As historian Michael Hunt put it: 'Vigor in acquiring new agricultural lands was essential to sustain a republican political economy in which individual opportunity, autonomy, and virtue might flourish. Without the addition of new lands, a territorially confined republic with a growing population would degenerate' (Hunt, 1987: 30).

Following the turmoil in Europe – the Napoleonic Wars, revolution, intensified industrialisation – the United States became the recipient of over four million immigrants from Europe, who transformed US city life and spread into the west, encouraged by a belief in Manifest Destiny to colonise North America. The belief was further perpetuated and sustained by the growing number of popular narratives on the glories of the expansion. With little in common, US nationalism, emerging simultaneously with European nationalism, took very different routes. In the United States 'the people' shared an imprecise vision of opportunity. Their orators often identified the 'imagined community' in terms of opposition to European identities. What 'one shared was a sense of an entirely new kind of country, uniquely marked by social, economic, and spatial *openness*' (Stephanson, 1995: 28, original italics). US nationalism had two strands to it. It became associated with the new ideologies that were informed by the narratives associated with the Founding Fathers, and perhaps most particularly with Thomas Jefferson's ideas on liberty, democracy and self-determination. Another vein of US nationalism, Louis Hartz wrote in the 1950s, was associated with the territorial state, strong and expansionist, which often contradicted the ideals and ideas associated with founding ideologies (Hartz, 1955: 189–90). The combination of the two, sometimes contradictory, sets of nationalism provided US statesmen with the option of referring to two traditions in its diplomacy: ideals and expansionism. Both of these attributes are present in US relations with Europe in the twentieth century.

Despite the abstract contradictions, despite the near destruction of the Union during the Civil War, despite questions of identity brought on by increased immigration, despite the removal and destruction of the Native American nations, the success of the United States, relative to that of the Soviet Union, and to that of Europe (united or not), was that it held together a nation the size of a continent (Reynolds, 1992: 256). In certain respects, by the turn of the nineteenth century various sectors of the US economy were not just rivalling their counterparts in certain European countries, they were rivalling the industrial output of the entire European continent. After the Civil War the United States was in a position to exploit its vast landmass for agriculture, raw materials and technological innovation. US growth following the Civil War was a phenomenon. Between 1865 and 1898 'wheat production increased by 256 per cent, corn by 222 per cent, refined sugar by 460 per cent, coal by 800 per cent, steel rails by 523 per cent', and so on (Kennedy, 1989: 312–13). Paul Kennedy suggests that there was an inevitability about the rise of US power. The United States enjoyed all the advantages with fewer disadvantages of the divided and nation-based economies of Europe.

Of course what this sort of productivity meant, especially prompted by the financial crises of the 1870s, was that Americans believed that they would have to compete with the European imperial powers for access to and acquisition of foreign markets. By the winter of 1884–85 the European powers met at the Berlin Conference on West Africa. Primarily they settled the regional boundaries and those of the Congo, but they also considered issues of navigation and trade. Though the United States was not actively involved in the territorial discussions it did have interests in the discussions on trade. 'In many ways,' Kennedy writes, 'the Berlin West Africa Conference can be seen symbolically, as the zenith of Old Europe's period of predominance in global affairs' (1989: 249). Even though the United States attended the conference, its views were not considered seriously and it did not participate in great power diplomacy until the 1890s.

The tremendous industrial output of the post-Civil War period pushed prices downward in the US economy, leading to what McCormick (1989) terms the 'Long Depression' of the 1880s and the 1890s. Government and 'Big Business' believed in the overproduction thesis, which suggested that a permanent industrial surplus in excess of the purchasing power of the domestic market would result in industrial strife which would in turn have to be met with state violence against worker unrest. As a result the state became increasingly active in the search for overseas markets to relieve domestic problems (McCormick, 1989: 18). Domestic US labour unrest, the so-called closing of the 'American Frontier' and the disappearance of foreign markets through European colonialism in Africa and Asia, impelled a more active US foreign policy towards the end of the nineteenth century.

The Spanish–American–Cuban War of 1898 projected the United States on to the world stage. In a very short period it had become an imperial in which European powers declined dramatically relative to the rising stock of the United States.

In the early part of the twentieth century the great powers were still predominantly European: Britain, France, Russia, Germany, Austria-Hungary and Italy. The United States did not enter European politicians' consciousness as a great power until the decisive contribution in the closing stages of the First World War. Of the European powers, Spain and Portugal, still imperial European nations, were not treated with the same gravity as the other great powers. Spain's reputation as a fighting power had suffered considerably after its decisive defeat by the United States. Even the British were considered to be somewhat on the 'downgrade' because they could not decisively put an end to the Boer War in South Africa. The United States drew great confidence from such circumstances, but still its diplomacy prior to the Great War remained regional and parochially concerned with its commercial interests in the Far East (Gardner, 1984: 26).

The world of European empires was coming to an end even though the European protagonists did not recognise the impending changes. With the rise of trade unionism and liberalism, the key agendas of the most powerful European states became dominated by domestic reform. In many ways the costs of such reform were funded through overseas expansion and the consolidation of colonial arrangements. As the historian Lloyd Gardner put it, 'to liberal imperialists on both sides of the Atlantic, domestic reform and foreign expansion went together' (Gardner, 1984: 20, 25).

The European balance of power was crucial to international stability, yet an increasing – if informal – compact between the United States and Britain was changing the conditions that had characterised the nineteenth century. Germany was the anomaly to the imperial network in the first half of the twentieth century. Imperialism provided European powers and the United States with a safety-valve for their domestic pressures. Yet German attempts, twice in the twentieth century, to expand its political influence through the acquisition of territory, to match its economic power, brought the world to points of catastrophe. Africa, Latin America, China and East Asia had become the colonies and domains of the other great powers. One of the twin features of the twentieth century has been the concurrent rise of German and US power. The German economy has risen to prominent positions three times. Once after unification in 1871, again under Nazi Germany and then again after the Second World War (Hobsbawm, 1994). After the turn of the century British businessmen were aware of the growth of a major German commercial and economic rival. Even though France still operated a vast colonial empire, it was intrinsically concerned with the reoccupation of Alsace and Lorraine, which Germany seized in 1871. France implicitly drew closer to Britain, to minimise imperial rivalry because its European interests were paramount. After the Boer War, Britain too cultivated a closer relationship with Washington. The new Anglo-American relationship permitted the British to remove their strategic power from the Western Hemisphere and also undermined the assumption on the part of nineteenth-century European statesmen that there would always be problems in the British-American relationship (Kennedy, 1989: 323).

Territorial colonialism and economic power were vital constituent parts of the great power diplomacy of the twentieth century. British hegemony was increasingly challenged by both the United States and by Germany. While Britain and the United States had expanded territorially, the British occupying vast portions of Africa and Asia and the Americans vast sections of the North American continent, the German challenge tried to incorporate both colonialism and continental conquest in the twentieth century (Arrighi, 1994: 58–60). As European rivalries played themselves out to their tragic end, the United States benefited considerably in relative terms with the decline of British and German power. The United States existed as a continent, it had a relative abundance of resources and an active state policy of assisting business abroad, maintaining open doors to trade where possible and closing their own market to competitive foreign products. 'By the time the struggle for world supremacy began, the US domestic economy was well on its way to being the new center of the world economy' (Arrighi, 1994: 61). The internal US capacity, coupled with the inter-European destruction, brought one of the most decisive changes to the structure of world power during the early twentieth century (Arrighi, 1994; Kennedy, 1989: 249–52). Throughout, US national interests were enhanced through the pursuit of economic opportunities, ideological ambitions and security concerns. The First World War was significant. The US economy boomed as a result of war orders, President Wilson promoted US ideologies in an attempt to shape the peace, and US security concerns were addressed through their participation in the war.

THE FIRST WORLD WAR: PRELUDE TO INTERVENTION, 1914–16

The literature on the origins of the First World War is huge. Needless to say there is no space here to expand on the issues (see Martel, 1996). Suffice it to say that, generally, German instability and perceived encirclement created tensions with the Allied Powers (Britain, France and Russia) and the Austrian rivalry with Russia over the Balkans provided the tinderbox for the war. On 28 June 1914 Archduke Francis Ferdinand was assassinated in Sarajevo. Within a month Austria-Hungary declared war on Serbia. Days later, on 1 August, Germany declared war on Russia in the east and invaded Luxembourg and Belgium on 2 and 4 August respectively. Britain, as a guarantor of Belgian neutrality, immediately declared war on Germany. Essentially, Europe divided between the Triple Alliance of France, Britain and Russia and the Central Powers of Germany and Austria-Hungary. Washington observed as Bulgaria and the Ottoman Empire soon joined the Central Powers. The Allies found support from Italy, Greece, Romania and Portugal. Japan entered the war, but stayed in the east, absorbing the former German colonial possessions. Within months battle lines had been drawn where the advancing armies met each other and dug trenches. Tragically, as Hobsbawn relates, 'they did not shift significantly for the next three and a half years' (1994: 24–5).

When war broke out Washington wanted no part of it. The pursuit of the various US national interests changed American attitudes towards the war over time. It is ironic that Wilson, elected on a largely domestic platform of reform, ended up as a 'foreign policy' president. With little knowledge of foreign affairs and perhaps because of his Presbyterian background and reformist inclinations, Wilson adopted a high moral tone to his foreign policy rhetoric. Despite his adventures in Mexico (1914–17), Wilson preached doctrines of self-determination, free trade, democratic expansion and the respect for law.

The European sphere, however, was different. When war broke out there Wilson was quick to request of Americans that they be 'neutral in fact as well as in name' and be 'impartial in thought as well as in action' [*Doc. 6*]. Ideally, Americans should not conduct any activities that favoured one side or the other, or that caused offence; otherwise the United States might be drawn into the war. Besides that, Wilson's electoral base was too precarious to upset substantial minorities within the United States. Though the vast majority of Americans favoured the Allies and especially the British, Wilson could not afford to alienate the substantial population of German-Americans (some eleven million), or the Irish- or the Scandinavian-Americans who also harboured grievances against the British and the Russians. The divisions over neutrality within the Wilson administration reflected the larger American social divisions on the US stance on the war. Though Colonel House and Robert Lansing advocated a more pro-British position, US opinion only changed as the more frequent and 'uncivilised' behaviour of the German U-boats was seen as detrimental to US interests. Americans had to be persuaded that the United States was playing a crucial role in the war, despite the official claims of neutrality. The war was having a dramatic impact on US culture and its economy. Eventually, the American public would come to accept and believe that their nation's power necessitated involvement in, and the leadership of, Europe. Wilson clearly intended to extend the US ideas associated with the progressive agenda. As Iriye puts it, reformers supporting Wilson 'considered the war a rare opportunity to carry on the task, for war required national unity and mobilization, an ideal condition for reorganizing domestic affairs'. New ideas on 'economic planning, public service, and public education on international events' were introduced (Iriye, 1993: 26–49). Thus, culturally, the United States was being drawn out of its traditional belief in isolation from the 'Old World' of Europe. Now there was a clear opportunity for America to extend its sphere of influence to encompass Europe, and US culture and ideology had to adjust to this new opportunity.

Initially, Wilson adhered to George Washington's advice in his farewell address of 1796: 'in extending our commercial relations to have with them as little political connection as possible' [*Doc. 2*]. American neutrality did not mean breaking relations with Europe during wartime. Commercial activities continued and opportunities were sought after. Financial transactions were completed; goods were transported on ships that flew the American flag. None of these activities was seen as a violation of the rights of the neutral United States. Indeed, they were considered beneficial. As the United States was experiencing a period of economic recession, they provided opportunities for growth and the extension of US business and finance into Europe. The United States took full opportunity. It entered the period of the First World War with a debt of $3.7 billion and surfaced in 1918 with a credit of $3.8 billion (LaFeber, 1989: 273).

Whatever the thoughts or intentions of the Wilson administration, neutrality made little sense under the circumstances. The German successes had hitherto been quite remarkable. Its troops were well into France and across Belgium, its armies had defeated Russian forces, and its U-boats were imposing considerable hardship on Britain through sinking supplies as they crossed the Atlantic. The sheer size of the US industrial capacity, the billions of dollars of Allied war orders, and the ability of the United States to produce the merchant ships that were rapidly being sunk made all the difference. US 'neutrality' favoured the Allies in terms of supplies and finance by a margin of ten to one (LaFeber, 1989: 273).

The Secretary of State, William Jennings Bryan, took exception to the pro-Allied type of neutrality that Wilson practised. He argued against the loans to the belligerents, but Wilson realised that the war was good for American prosperity and the national interest required such economic recovery. Bryan was in the minority within the cabinet. Most were on the Allied side culturally as well as materially, and British navel power swung the balance. It 'cut US exports to Germany from $169 million to only $2 million annually' and during the first two years of the war US sales to the Allied powers quadrupled, alleviating the effects of the recession in the United States (Bagby, 1999: 23).

By 1915 Britain had blockaded Germany and the Germans in turn declared that the waters around the British Isles were a war zone. They began using U-boats to interdict merchant and passenger ships bound to replenish Allied supplies. The US insistence on its rights as a neutral state to sail through war zones unimpeded brought it into diplomatic conflict with both Britain and Germany. Anglo-American relations were close to breaking point when Germany sunk the British passenger liner the *Lusitania* off the southern Irish coast in May 1915. With over 1,000 casualties, of which 128 were American, the United States insisted on German reparations and its renunciation of submarine warfare. Germany was quick to issue its regrets, fearful of drawing the United States into the war. Secretary of State Bryan resigned because the United States insisted on neutrality rights in such circumstances. Still, the incident was not enough to bring the United States into war. Internal disagreements persisted over the morality of the German U-boat activities and the attempt by the British Navy to starve the German nation into submission. Aware of the effects of its U-boat activities on the US administration and public opinion, Germany refrained from sinking passenger liners for a brief period of time between the sinking of the *Arabic* in August 1915 to the sinking of the *Sussex* in March 1916.

Following Bryan's resignation the issue began to fade. The new Secretary of State, Robert Lansing, was much more pro-British than his predecessor was, and thus there was little further dissent within the cabinet. The United States edged closer to Britain. US opinion, too, changed in reaction to German tactics, aided by an extensive British propaganda campaign that convinced most Americans that the Central Powers were undemocratic enemies of civilisation.

In the movement towards Britain, Wilson employed the services of his friend and advisor, Colonel Edward House, who did not hold any official position within the government. In the spring of 1915 House travelled to London to promote certain terms for the peace. Yet his limited suggestions were considered inadequate given the millions that had died to date. By February 1916 House signed the House–Grey Memorandum with the British Foreign Secretary, Sir Edward Grey. The gist of the memorandum was that the United States would call a peace conference at a time of its convenience, benefiting the Allied Powers. If the Germans refused to participate, the United States would enter the war on the side of the Allies. If the Germans accepted, but then did not accept the terms at the conference, the United States would again enter the war on the side of the Allies. In either eventuality the United States indicated that it would 'probably' join the Allied cause.

Still, Wilson had to remain somewhat cautious. 1916 was an election year and he could not afford to alienate the significant Irish or German vote. His administration campaigned on the slogan: 'He kept us out of war'. As it was, Wilson's victory was narrow. But once returned to office in November 1916, the shackles of public opinion were removed and his administration was free to determine the US course towards war.

By the turn of the year three significant developments led the United States closer to war. First, in January, Germany announced its resumption of unrestricted U-boat activity and promptly began sinking both British and American ships. Wilson was convinced that the German Admiralty had greater influence over the government and that they probably would not turn to the negotiating table voluntarily. Such militarism had to be defeated (Iriye, 1993: 40). Second, Washington obtained an intercepted message from the German Foreign Secretary, Alfred Zimmerman, to the Mexican government, offering to form an alliance and the possibility of recovering half the Mexican territory that had been lost to the United States in the 1846–48 war. The publication of the telegram helped to galvanise US public opinion in support of the war effort. Finally, in March 1917 the Russian Revolution removed the tsarist regime, which was replaced by a reformist government under Alexander Kerensky. With the removal of the tsar the autocrats of Europe were clearly in opposition and on the side of the Central Powers. Wilson could now present the war in much more grandiose and universalistic terms.

During the initial years of the war, Washington benefited economically through the disproportionate trade with the Allies, which served the US economy and began to lift it out of recession. The legalistic position adopted on neutrality preserved a semblance of US security interests for a time, but also allowed them to position themselves above the war. However, should the United States remain out of the war, the opportunity to extend its sphere of influence in Europe would be similarly limited.

US INTERVENTION

In January 1917 Wilson called for 'a peace without victory'. In a speech before the US Senate he outlined his vision for a just and lasting peace. He argued that there could not just be a return to the old order: '... only a tranquil Europe can be a stable Europe. There must be, not a balance of power, but a community of power; not organised rivalries, but an organized common peace.' The speech heralded a shift away from the realism and systems of alliances that characterised nineteenth-century European diplomacy to a system that has come to be known as Wilsonian internationalism, ushering in collective security. In January 1917, he argued, somewhat prophetically, that a peace of the victor against the vanquished would not endure: 'Victory would mean peace forced upon the loser, a victor's terms imposed upon the vanquished. It would be accepted in humiliation, under duress, at an intolerable sacrifice, and would leave a sting, a resentment, a bitter memory upon which terms of peace would rest, not permanently, but only upon quicksand' [*Doc. 7*]. Yet, within months, Washington had thrown its power on to the side of the Allies and participated in that very outcome.

The United States did not enter the war as an Allied Power, but as an 'associated' one. Even though after the revolution Russia could be considered a democratic state, the European Allies were still colonial powers, which Wilson objected to in principle. Moreover, he shared Vladimir Lenin's belief that the war in Europe was an attempt to maintain capital within Europe and their various colonies in Asia and Africa. So, despite siding with the Allies, in his war address to Congress, Wilson articulated the US differences as well. The war was cast as an attempt to reshape the world order. On 2 April 1917, Wilson informed Congress and the American people that neutrality had not been enough. Now the Germans had initiated unrestricted U-boat activity and Americans were increasingly among the victims. Though the war was against Germany and its government, Wilson pointed out, 'we act without animus, not in enmity towards [the German] people...'. Wilson used the message to introduce concepts that would affect the subsequent debates on international relations throughout the rest of the century. It would be a war for the 'liberation of [the world's] peoples', 'for the rights of nations great and small and the privilege of men everywhere to choose their way of life and of obedience. The world must be made safe for democracy.' Wilson went on to explain that the United States was not serving its selfish ends; it sought 'no conquest, no dominion', or any indemnities or material compensation, but 'we are but one of the champions of the rights of mankind' [*Doc. 8*].

Wilson's vision seemed somewhat extraordinary to the European leaders grounded in realism and the pursuit of their national interests. David Lloyd George, the British Prime Minister, and Georges Clemenceau, the French Prime Minister, found US rhetoric rather odd, though they appreciated US assistance in terms of the material supplies and its forces. They surmised that their differences could and would be sorted out later around the negotiating tables of Versailles.

Wilson's vision has had an enduring impact not only among US policymakers, but also among many of the international institutions that have existed through the latter half of the twentieth century. His ideas were especially influential in the creation of the United Nations and the International Monetary Fund, which have promoted a certain conception of an international liberal economic order. In 1917 Wilson promoted self-determination, recognising that nationalism was a powerful sentiment. Indeed, nationalism would almost immediately bring down the Ottoman, Russian and Austro-Hungarian empires, and it would also contribute to the demise of the European colonial empires after the Second World War. It was an irony of US foreign relations, however, that Wilson's vision of self-determination was largely limited to the European world. When a young nationalist, later known as Ho Chi Minh, approached the Wilson delegation in Paris searching for support for Indochinese self-determination against French occupation, he was rebuffed.

Further, Wilson believed that democracy was the only form of legitimate government and that US policy should promote it. He assumed democracy and capitalism were mutually beneficial and reinforcing concepts. In addition, he believed that an increased respect for international law was necessary, that the global economic order would need to be characterised by non-discrimination and an open, anti-protectionist market and, finally, that a system of collective security, instead of the balance of power, was needed to maintain a lasting peace (T. Smith, 1994: 85–6). In short, Wilsonian ideology projected a stable, orderly, liberal-democratic internationalism that sought to avoid the extremes of revolution and reaction. It was a new and global ideology that sought a middle road through European imperialism and the revolutionary activities of Russia, Mexico and China.

There was a considerable delay between the announcement of war against Germany and the actual arrival of US forces. Prior to the US declaration of war it had benefited enormously from the increased orders from Europe – an economic situation that in fact pulled the United States out of debt. The preparations for war increased economic activity and prosperity. The emerging symbiotic relationship between business, government and the military cast long shadows throughout the twentieth century. Mobilisation enhanced these relationships, where Wilson had earlier sought to limit them. The war saw increased production throughout the economy. African-Americans moved north to fill the factories and women moved increasingly into employed labour to meet wartime requirements. The war boosted profits and wages. It benefited the progressive political economy. It 'strengthened the cooperative planning ethic within business and government. It also sped the transformation in civil–military relations that modern warfare made necessary and introduced the idea and practice of industrial preparedness' (Koistinen, 1997: 297). US entry into the war clearly served its national interests, defined around the three areas of economic opportunity, ideological influence and enhanced security.

THE RUSSIAN REVOLUTION

Initially the Russian Revolution pleased Washington and served its national interests concerning its position in the war, but as the revolution became increasingly radical and as Russia withdrew from the war, US antagonism rose. Wilson applauded the Russian Revolution shortly after the tsar abdicated on 15 March 1917. As the Russian Constituent Assembly began its meetings, the broad indications of greater democracy suited Wilson's ideological ambitions. The war effort could be presented henceforth as a fight between the democracies and the autocrats of Europe. Effusively, Wilson asked whether 'the wonderful and heartening things that have been happening' in Russia did not give all Americans assurance and hope for the future. A-historically, he proceeded, 'Russia was known by those who knew it best to have been always in fact democratic at heart, in all the vital habits of her thought ... and [now] the great, generous Russian people have added in all their naïve majesty and might to the forces that are fighting for freedom in the world, for justice, and for peace. Here is a fit partner for a League of Honour' (Wilson, quoted in Shaw, 1924: 379). Wilson saw Russia as vitally important for the post-war order. The democratic states could enhance international justice and outmanoeuvre the European colonial powers.

Advisors urged Wilson to recognise Russia formally. Its psychological impact would be tremendous; America would outstretch 'a welcoming hand to the world's newest liberal revolution from the oldest'. In fact Washington was the first to recognise the Provisional Government on 22 March 1917. The recognition, however, was delayed until it was certain that the Russians would stay in the war (Gardner, 1984: 133–4). Economic aid was provided too, but only $188 million of the $450 million allocated was used before Alexander Kerensky was overthrown in November (Gaddis, 1990: 61).

As Washington sought further engagement with Russia through aid and efforts towards further integration, Kerensky was losing control. In mid-June Russian forces began an offensive in the south, yet a widespread refusal to obey orders by the Russian troops undermined Kerensky. General Lavr Kornilov insisted that the offensive be curtailed and was appointed the commander-in-chief of the Russian forces. Days later, in early July, another offensive was launched in the north. Initial success soon turned to failure. The consequent social unrest and rioting was put down forcefully by troops loyal to Kerensky. Having arrested and hounded the Bolsheviks through the summer, Kerensky was forced to rely on their support by late summer to avert a coup from the right organised by Kornilov. The Kornilov Affair provided the Bolsheviks with greater power. They obtained a majority in the Moscow Soviet by late September. Leon Trotsky became chairman of the Moscow Soviet in early October and the Bolsheviks initiated an armed rising. By 7 November 1917 the Bolsheviks seized power. Land was trans-ferred to the people, factories were seized and handed over to the workers and the moderate left was suppressed. Kerensky fled to the United States. Germany and Russia began negotiations in Brest-Litovsk on concluding a separate peace.

Lenin and Trotsky's radicalism alarmed and divided Washington. Their call for world revolution and Trotsky's suggestions that self-determination would not be granted to the Allies' colonies created divisions and frustrated the attempts to convince the Russians not to sign a separate peace with the Germans. The success of the revolution depended in large part on extracting Russia from the war. The Bolsheviks were manoeuvring the Wilson adminis-tration into what seemed to be a difficult choice. Either the war was fought for self-determination, which should be universally applied, or it was not. Yet on the other hand Wilson abhorred the Bolshevik take-over and the lost hopes of his vision for a liberal democratic order. The Bolshevik revolution was considered chaotic and anarchic, the antithesis of Wilson's conception of order. Wilson's advisors were divided on how best to respond. Secretary of State Lansing wanted to send in US troops, yet Colonel Edward House urged keeping the Russians in the war.

Bolshevik rhetoric was widely considered an attack on civilisation in Wilson's inner circles. The prospect of world revolution was anathema to Washington. Reacting to Trotsky's pronouncements on self-determination of late December 1917, Lansing wrote to Wilson that 'the document is an appeal to the proletariat of all countries, to the ignorant and mentally deficient, who by their numbers are urged to become masters. Here seems to me to lie a very real danger in view of the present social unrest throughout the world' (quoted in Gardner, 1984: 161). The famous Fourteen Points announced by Wilson on 8 January 1918 was an attempt both to restate US war aims and counter the Bolshevik appeal and to form the specific terms of peace for any subsequent negotiation. They were also designed to keep the Russians from concluding a separate peace with the Germans.

The key points included advocating 'open covenants of peace' and 'no private international understandings of any kind', and 'absolute freedom of navigation upon the seas'. Point three was crucial for US commerce and economic integration: it called for 'the removal ... of all economic barriers and the establishment of equality of trade conditions'. Point four proposed guarantees of arms reductions. Point five alarmed the West European powers, calling for 'a free, open-minded, and absolutely impartial adjustment of all colonial claims'. Point six was crucial for keeping the Russians in the war, requesting an evacuation of all Russian territory. The remaining points dealt mainly with issues of territorial integrity and control. Finally, the fourteenth point, Wilson's cherished idea, called for 'a general association of nations' or the basis of what would later become the League of Nations [*Doc. 9*].

The ideological rivalry between the United States and Russia that characterised the rest of the 'short twentieth century' began in earnest during this period. As Cassels writes, 'to the war weary millions Lenin and Wilson appeared as alternative messiahs, and indeed since 1917 each had been projecting himself as a saviour from outside Europe' (1996: 139). In many ways these ideologies were replacing the conceptual notions of European monarchy and absolutism. But with the ideological competition between Wilsonianism and Leninism there was also the battle for the 'hearts and minds' of the world at large. The ideologies were anti-imperial, both sought peace and promoted self-determination, and they both promoted a form of national development based on their own experiences (Clark, 1997: 64). Despite these similarities the differences were obviously stark as well. Soviet socialist economic structures were anathema to the United States, and their ideological conceptions of democracy were obviously very different. In fact, the similarities could really only be considered in terms of opposition to the old autocracies of Central Europe and the colonial systems of Western Europe.

Even though Lenin allowed Wilson's points to be widely circulated in Russia, they did not have the desired immediate effect. On 3 March 1918 Russia concluded the much-interrupted negotiations and signed the Brest-Litovsk Treaty with Germany. With it Russia withdrew from the war, which allowed the Germans to transfer more troops to the western front. Nevertheless, German forces continued to capture territory from the Russians and by July 1918 Wilson sent US forces into Russia to assist the White Russians in the civil war. US battalions were sent in through Murmansk in the north and Vladivostok in the east. US–Soviet hostility remained a defining context for Washington's relations with the rest of Europe until 1991.

THE WESTERN FRONT AND WESTERN PEACE

American forces began to arrive in Western Europe in the summer of 1917 and engaged in relatively minor actions until the summer of 1918 when they launched offensives at Aisne-Marne in July, and St Michel and Meuse-Argonne in September. The US productive capacity, however, made a crucial difference. It provided the Allies with billions of dollars and abundant material assistance. It provided the ships (merchant and naval), equipment, food and eventually a force of fresh men. For Paul Kennedy, 'In terms of economic power, therefore, the entry of the United States into the war quite transformed the balances, and more than compensated for the collapse of Russia at the same time' (Kennedy, 1989: 349–50).

The American Expeditionary Force complicated the failed final German offensive after the spring of 1918. During the summer of 1918 the fruits of nationalism and self-determination were evident in the Allied recognition of Czechoslovakia, which contributed to the crumbling Central European empires by that autumn. Yugoslavia gained independence in October and an armistice was signed with the Ottoman Empire on 30 October; on 3 November an armistice was signed with Austria-Hungary.

During October the Germans had explored the opportunities of laying down their weapons on the basis of Wilson's Fourteen Points. In the west they had not been clearly defeated on the field of battle: their armies remained within France until the eventual armistice was signed at the eleventh hour on the eleventh day of the eleventh month of 1918, when they began to march home.

Though Wilson put forward the Fourteen Points as the terms of peace, they were far too general to address the specifics in Europe and they met with resistance from both the British and the French. Moreover, before the United States would accept the German surrender, they insisted that the Kaiser abdicate; they would not negotiate unless there was a republican government. Though William II initially balked, Germany eventually proclaimed a republic on 9 November 1918.

Wilson and Lenin were seen by many in Europe as the new saviours from the east and the west. Indeed, when Wilson arrived in Europe he was greeted everywhere with adulating crowds. He was seen as one of the most popular men in Europe. The British had been wary of the new American power for some time. In 1916 the British Chancellor of the Exchequer thought 'by next June, or earlier, the President of the American Republic would be in a position, if he wishes, to dictate his terms to us' (Kennedy, 1989: 346). And in Washington there was a similar sentiment. In 1917 Wilson told House: 'When the war is over, we can force [England and France] to our way of thinking, because by that time they will be financially in our hands' (LaFeber, 1989: 297). But these visions of grandeur turned out to be illusions. The British resisted the point on the freedom of the seas and the French resisted the idea of a peace without victory. They were intent, having suffered the most casualties, to disarm Germany and incapacitate its military power. So even before the peace negotiations commenced Wilson was beginning to encounter resistance. The United States, after all, had not endured the same suffering as the Europeans. With some ten million dead and another five million wounded, the Europeans were bound to pursue their national interests, their national security and *realpolitik* over and above what appeared to be Wilson's idealistic points.

Wilson had prepared badly for Paris. The Democratic campaign in 1918 was counterproductive, handing a majority to the Republicans in the Senate. Henry Cabot Lodge, no friend of Wilson's, now chaired the key Senate Foreign Relations Committee. Moreover, for such a momentous set of negotiations, Wilson did not take any senior Republicans to Paris, yet they were dominant in the body that would have to ratify the treaty that he obtained around the negotiating table. In addition, his prolonged stay in Europe undermined Wilson's domestic political support.

In Paris the negotiating process with twenty-seven states was too large and unwieldy to make progress. It was soon limited to ten members, the ministers or presidents and their secretaries from the United States, Britain, France, Italy and Japan. Eventually even that group was considered too big so the Japanese left and the secretaries were dismissed. The key negotiators were Woodrow Wilson, David Lloyd George, Georges Clemenceau and Vittorio Orlando. Here Wilson got into trouble. The British economist, John Meynard Keynes, later wrote about his relative slowness compared to the others. His attention to detail was inadequate; he constantly wanted to discuss the League of Nations, which was not that important to the Europeans compared to the real issues of disarmament, reparations, dismemberment of the empires, and Germany's acceptance of responsibility for the war. Wilson's ambitions did not fit comfortably with European *realpolitik* [Doc. 10].

and by extending the necessary credit to Germany the economic system was allowed to function for a time. The initiative provided several lessons for the post-Second World War period. The Dawes solution was to arrange a $100 million loan from J. P. Morgan to Germany and a reduction of the annual reparations, which eased the situation in Germany and allowed the cycle of reparations and repayments to the US banks to resume. Washington applied considerable pressure on Morgan to provide the loans, which belied the idea that these were private solutions. The interactive relationship between bankers and the state emerged into patterns of symbiotic relations that enhanced US foreign policy and business opportunities. Corporations benefited extensively from what Rosenberg characterises as the US 'co-operative state'. US integration and finance assisted German development and reconciliation. From the Dawes Plan to the Wall Street Crash of 1929 Germany was the most attractive place for US investors, providing about '80 percent of the capital borrowed by German credit institutions' (Rosenberg, 1982: 150–1).

The 'co-operative' spirit extended to further banking arrangements with European states as the three Republican administrations urged other banks to act as stabilising forces in Europe. With the short-term solution to the German reparations problem and the restoration of confidence aided by the other banks, most Europeans moved back to the gold standard between 1925 and 1928. The struggle between Britain and the United States over whose currency would be the premier unit of exchange in international commerce continued, however. Economic stability was all-important and the Coolidge administration regarded the banking initiatives in the national interest. Secretary of the Treasury, Andrew Mellon, argued that the return to the gold standard would stabilise the economies of Europe and increase their purchasing power, which 'means a greater demand for our surplus products' (cited in Rosenberg, 1982: 153).

ECONOMIC FRAGMENTATION: THE WALL STREET CRASH AND THE GREAT DEPRESSION

Though the United States remained somewhat politically isolated from Europe throughout the inter-war period, its economy turned from its internationalist engagement through the post-war decade to an inward-looking nationalism after 1929. Economic internationalism accentuated the boom of the 1920s. By that time the United States accounted for 40% of global industrial production, 16% of international trade and 50% of its gold reserves. This vast disproportion between the development of the United States and that of Europe meant that Washington and New York continued to act as a stabilising force for European economic recovery. In June 1929 the Young Plan provided for further reductions in German reparations and

European repayments, but it no sooner came into effect than the Wall Street Crash of October 1929 undermined its stabilising efforts. As thousands of banks closed, businesses went bankrupt and unemployment rose from 1.5 million to 12 million between 1929 and 1932, US exports and imports dropped dramatically by some 70%. Given the continental size of the United States, Americans did not rely on external economic connections to the same extent that the European powers relied on the transatlantic trade, not to mention trade with their colonies. The sheer differences in size and the European dependency meant that the crash and subsequent depression had considerable effects throughout the world (Iriye, 1993: 116; Hobsbawm, 1994: 99).

With little US capital available for foreign investment the liberal internationalist capitalist system collapsed. Multilateral trade shrank dramatically, currency convertibility and the relatively free capital movements virtually ceased, bringing economic growth to a standstill. President Hoover reacted tardily to the crash. He believed in the free market and business solutions, not governmental intervention. Nevertheless, the economic crisis pushed Congress to seek national economic solutions. In an attempt to bolster US businesses in 1930 Congress passed the Smoot–Hawley tariff, in effect building an economic wall around the United States. By 1931 European tariff rates were raised by 66%. World trade shrank from $30.3 million to $20.3 million simultaneously. Hoover imposed a moratorium on repayments for a year, but the action was still not sufficient to regain market confidence and soon Germany foreclosed on its reparations and Britain and France ceased debt repayments to the United States. By 1932 several European countries, and crucially Britain, abandoned the gold standard (Iriye, 1993: 118; Brands, 1994: 104).

In 1933 the sixty-four nations convened at the London Economic Conference searched for a formula that would restore the international economy by stabilising currencies, renewing loans and renegotiating debt payments. President Roosevelt (1933–45) refused to address this question, arguing that it suited the European nations more than the United States. The economic nationalism that characterised the rest of the decade was cemented when Roosevelt rejected the proposal of currency stabilisation and convertibility, which scuttled the London Conference. Instead, in June 1934, Congress passed the Reciprocal Trade Agreement Act, which created a series of bilateral agreements in which tariffs would be reduced on certain products.

Over the next few years the world economy fragmented into a series of closed blocs. Each state chose to protect its own economy first, which further exacerbated the decline in trade. These blocs raised high tariff barriers against their competitors and sought to restrict trade within the bloc, thus alleviating the costs associated with external trade and the free currency convertibility. They engaged in economic exchange often through barter to avoid the declining terms of trade, especially for the extraction and manufacture of raw materials.

East European states reacted to the Depression by introducing protectionist measures and resorting to barter as the only viable form of trade. Their markets had disappeared, they were heavily in debt and they had no access to international credit. The US tariffs of 1930 signalled an international trend that impacted on Europe: *protect the domestic economy first.* By 1932 the British compounded the situation by setting up the imperial preference system in Ottawa, making US trade with Britain or its colonies less attractive and impractical. Germany's economic system focused inward under the Nazis as they withdrew from the fragmenting world economy, engaged in barter, and created a more exclusive economic area with the Central and East Europeans. German economic independence was confirmed in 1936 with its Four-Year Plan. Soviet Russia too had formed a closed bloc, but unlike the rest of Europe it enjoyed considerable economic growth rates, averaging around 10%. Such growth at the height of the western economic depression severely challenged the philosophical assumptions that underpinned the capitalist system.

When Franklin Roosevelt took office in March 1933 his inauguration made clear that the US focus would be inward. 'International relations' were deemed important, but not the key priority. His primary focus would be to establish 'a sound national economy'. Unlike his predecessor, Roosevelt believed that further state intervention was absolutely necessary to bring the United States out of depression. Some Republicans and internationalists considered his New Deal heretical to both business and individualism. Former President Hoover even wondered whether the New Deal had been infected from the 'original stream of fascism' (Gardner, 1993: 25).

The United States finally extended diplomatic recognition to Russia in 1933. Previously it had refused to do so because of the dictatorial characteristics of the government and because it refused to repay tsarist debts. However, in a time of depression, recognition promised increased trade, although few benefits resulted.

WASHINGTON AND THE RISE OF FASCIST EUROPE

At the same time as Joseph Stalin rose to power in the Soviet Union, a series of fascist movements gained influence and then power from the early 1920s into the 1930s, which appeared to threaten war between the various blocs and challenged US ideas of liberal-democratic capitalism. In 1923 Benito Mussolini acquired dictatorial power following a struggle with the Italian Communists. Though Italy had fought on the Allied side in the First World

War, it had not benefited from the war and fascism seemed to provide the answers through increased production, military spending and promises by Mussolini to restore the might of Italy around the Mediterranean, rejuvenating the Roman Empire. In Germany, by 1932 the Nazis had gained the greatest number of seats in the *Reichstag* and by January 1933 Adolph Hitler had assumed power as Chancellor. Hitler was bent on restoring Germany's reputation and power after the First World War. He did not accept the war guilt clause or, indeed, that Germany had lost the war. He pulled Germany out of depression through the rapid introduction of public works, re-militarisation and by dramatically increasing industrial output to rival and eventually surpass that of Britain. Finally, in 1936, General Francisco Franco initiated the Spanish Civil War against the government that lasted into 1939. Troops from Italy and arms from Nazi Germany assisted his forces.

These three fascist governments in Europe (together with the rise of Japan in Asia) threatened the US vision of reviving the international economy by maintaining closed blocs and by their anti-liberal politics. Germany and Italy addressed their economic grievances through territorial expansion. They considered themselves great powers, but unlike the United States, the Soviet Union, Britain and France, German colonial possessions had been taken after the First World War. Now they believed that they had inadequate areas under their control to develop resources, exploit markets and trade. The Americans had the continent of North America, the Soviets had East Asia, and the French and British had colonies all over the world. Hitler looked for *lebensraum* or living space to achieve his vision of a German *Reich* that would last, he said, for a thousand years.

Washington increasingly saw a threat from these powers as they began to occupy larger areas of Europe and Asia. Such moves contracted markets and the economic living spaces for the British, French and Americans. From 1935 Italy moved into Ethiopia and in 1936 it formed the Axis with Germany, which then also began its expansion into vast areas of Europe. US national interests eventually demanded a response. European conflagration threatened US security and economic prosperity, and the rise of fascism presented yet another ideology with which to contend.

US ISOLATION?

The United States under Roosevelt initially maintained a somewhat isolationist stance towards European affairs. In 1934 the Nye Committee, which was investigating the causes of US entry into the First World War, concluded that it was bankers, arms manufacturers and propaganda that had brought the United States into war, not the violations of neutrality or the attacks on US ships. US public opinion wanted very little to do with

European affairs; Americans did not want to be duped into a second major war. Between 1935 and 1937 Congress passed three Neutrality Acts which severely restricted the options open to Roosevelt [*Doc. 14*]. To avoid another situation such as that of the First World War, arms could not be shipped to belligerents. In 1936 this was extended to loans and credits. Though he later overcame the provisions of the Acts, in his first term in office he adhered to the isolationist sentiment and his response to Axis expansion remained verbal. Roosevelt abhorred Nazi Germany and criticised its treatment of Jews and the policies on race more generally. But even as the American government condemned such German policies the United States refused to increase the immigration quotas for Jewish people (Iriye, 1993: 144) and US business remained intimately tied to Nazi Germany.

During his second term in office Roosevelt sought more freedom from the Neutrality Acts and increasingly realised that the United States could not remain aloof from the impending war. In 1937 Roosevelt invited British Prime Minister Neville Chamberlain to Washington to explore the possibilities of cooperation. Chamberlain's now infamous rejection indicated: 'It is always best and safest to count on nothing from the Americans but words' (Iriye, 1993: 157). Nevertheless, Roosevelt continued his attempt to re-engage US power in the increasingly threatening atmosphere. His speech of October 1937, calling for a quarantine against the 'epidemic of world lawlessness', signalled the beginnings of a more active policy that would eventually lead to the visions encapsulated in the Atlantic Charter of August 1941 (Hunt, 1987: 147).

Between Chamberlain's dismissal of the American assistance in 1938 and Churchill's signature of the Charter in 1941 lay a series of manoeuvres that brought the United States out of political isolation from European affairs to the position, as Roosevelt described it, as the 'arsenal of democracy'. First, Chamberlain grew increasingly worried about US intentions. Roosevelt had called for a consideration of the 'inequities' of the Versailles Treaty that enraged Hitler. Chamberlain was worried that the United States was again trying to bring about a multilateral economic agreement, possibly without the British, if the Axis powers accepted. Moreover, any reconsideration of Versailles would include a German demand for the return of its colonies. Chamberlain viewed this attempt at multilateral appeasement as a threat to British commercial and colonial interests and chose instead to follow a policy of bilateral appeasement in September 1938. As Gardner explains, 'Appeasement ... might rescue Britain from unwanted entanglements across the Atlantic' (1993: 18), but the British were not about to abandon the imperial preference system or redraw the colonial map to suit US and German interests. So in September 1938 Chamberlain opted for 'peace in our time'. At the Munich Conference Britain and France agreed that Hitler could occupy a part of Czechoslovakia if the remaining territory was respected. Given that the United States was still experiencing the Depression, it did not want to begin hostilities with Germany and thus, following Munich, Roosevelt sent a very brief cable to Chamberlain: 'Good Man' (Schulzinger, 1990: 164). Ironically, it was ultimately the war, and wartime production, rather than the New Deal, that pulled the United States out of depression.

Hitler took the rest of Czechoslovakia within the year, leading future politicians and historians to draw the 'lessons' of Munich: that aggression should never be appeased and should be countered immediately. By May 1939 Roosevelt initiated the idea of 'cash and carry'. He proposed that European belligerents be allowed to purchase US goods so long as they paid in cash and sailed to the United States to collect them; this would benefit the Allies yet keep the United States out of the war. Nevertheless, the Senate, believing that Roosevelt's proposal would draw the United States into the war, initially rejected it. When Germany invaded Poland in September 1939 and Britain and France declared war, there was a slight shift in United States sentiment. Though most Americans favoured the Allies, there was still very little public inclination to join the war. Ultimately, in November, Congress passed the cash and carry proposal, which obviously favoured the Allies, given the disparity of power in the merchant and marine fleets of the belligerent powers.

THE SECOND WORLD WAR

The traditional interpretation of the Second World War hides many of the divisions that existed among the Allies. Of course the primary objectives were to defeat the Axis powers in both Europe and Asia, though divisions among the Allies were rarely far beneath the surface. First, between 1939 and 1941, there were attempts to induce the United States into the war while still maintaining the exclusive British economic system and the European colonial empires, both of which Washington opposed. Beyond the specific war aims of seeking the total surrender of the Axis forces, there was considerable acrimony on the future shape of the post-war world order. Second, the traditional interpretations of the Second World War as the 'Good War' have tended to ignore the US reaction to the Holocaust and the pursuit of its national interests during the war. Third, there were considerable disagreements on the grand strategies to be employed in the war. The results of the particular set of strategies chosen had a deep impact on the subsequent Cold War. And last, the importance of the war and its boost to the economy, finally pulling the United States out of depression, needs to be more fully acknowledged, because of the impact on subsequent US strategies in Europe.

By the time Paris fell to the Nazis in June 1940 Roosevelt was intent on assisting the Allies with material aid, though Congress was still reluctant to join the war. Roosevelt realised that the world was shrinking and that the vast oceans to its east and west no longer provided adequate security in the impending age of airpower. Such spatial contraction limited US options to remain 'isolated' from European affairs. He understood and explained this during his pan-American address on 14 April 1939: 'Beyond question, within a scant few years air fleets will cross the ocean as easily as today they cross the closed European seas. Economic functioning of the world becomes increasingly a unit; no interruption of it anywhere can fail, in the future, to disrupt economic life everywhere' (Commager, 1963: 414–15). By January 1941 his State of the Union speech linked US security, democracy and business with 'events far beyond our borders'. The most immediate task was to become the 'arsenal for democracy' based around the Four Freedoms: of speech, of worship, from want and from fear. The principles were largely incorporated in the Atlantic Charter of August 1941 [*Doc. 15*]. After the tripartite pact between Germany, Italy and Japan had been signed in September 1940 Washington grew more alarmed. By early 1941 Roosevelt's solution to British requests for aid came in the form of the Lend-Lease Bill, in which the United States would lend Britain US destroyers in return for the lease of islands for US military bases across the British Empire. The bill was passed with significant majorities in Congress in March 1941. The $7 billion programme had to be protected from German U-boat activity and so US warships were deployed across half of the Atlantic without congressional approval. The US fleet engaged in search missions for the Royal Navy. By April the United States had included Greenland as a US protectorate as well as the tiny islands in the Azores group off the west coast of Spain. By July US troops were moved into Iceland, not only to ensure further security for sea lanes of communication, but to relieve the British troops who could be deployed elsewhere (LaFeber, 1989: 376–7). Secretly, the United States had become an active participant in the war even before any formal declarations were made or the Japanese had attacked Pearl Harbor.

Hitler was cautious not to provoke the Americans. If they entered the war, he thought the Japanese would keep them occupied in the Pacific. The Japanese war with the Soviets and the Nazi-Soviet Pact kept Stalin's forces at bay for a time. But in April 1941 the Japanese signed an agreement with the Soviets. Hitler's short-term strategies came to nought. In June 1941, in what many regard as his primary mistake, Hitler invaded the Soviet Union, taking some pressure off the western front and allowing the Allies time to regroup and receive further US aid. US and European power contracted in the east as the Japanese moved south and pushed the French out of Indochina, the British from Malaya and Singapore and the Americans from the Philippines prior to their strike at Pearl Harbor.

Despite its cultural affinity with the British in particular, the United States could not fight on the side of colonial powers, whose conduct went against US ideologies and its assumed traditions. Although the main goal of the war was to defeat the Axis powers, Roosevelt also wanted to set out the agenda for the post-war world order, and to cast a more positive light on US involvement in the war. Thus, in August 1941, when Roosevelt and Churchill met off the coast of Newfoundland to agree on war aims, Roosevelt used the meeting to announce US ideological interests to the world. Churchill expected an immediate US entry into the war and the maintenance of British interests. The resulting eight-point charter included three points with references to political self-determination: territorial adjustments should not be made without the consent of the governed and that all peoples should have the right to choose the form of government under which they would live. This, coupled with the fourth point that all states should have equal access 'to the trade and to the raw materials of the world which are needed for their economic prosperity', roused Churchill's ire. He eventually managed to insert the phrase 'with due respect for their existing obligation' to exempt the British Empire, but Roosevelt was also able to insist that India become a signatory to the Charter [*Doc. 16*]. Despite these disagreements, Churchill was assured that Roosevelt would participate in the war in an increasingly provocative manner without actually declaring war. Roosevelt told Churchill that 'everything was to be done to force an "incident" that could lead to war' (LaFeber, 1989: 382). Though unrelated to the provocative US efforts in the Atlantic, the Japanese raid on Pearl Harbor solved Roosevelt's problem. The following day the British and the Americans declared war on Japan, and on 11 December Germany and Italy in turn declared war on the United States.

The Grand Alliance, formed in early 1942, brought the United States together with a range of European nations. The combination of the United States, Great Britain and the Soviet Union formed an alliance of liberal-democratic capitalism, British imperialism and communism. Their only common purpose was to destroy Hitler's New European Order. US productive capacity made a decisive difference. In spite of Japan's initial successes, it was bound to be defeated in the long run, and in the West US material and munitions eventually tipped the balance in favour of the Grand Alliance. 'Manufacturing output doubled between 1940 and 1943', US arms production rose by eight times 'to a level nearly that of Britain, the Soviet Union, and Germany combined'. The figures for the production of ships and aircraft are similarly impressive; the supply of trains and vehicles ran into the hundreds of thousands, shipped to Britain and the Soviet Union under lend-lease. By the end of the war the United States accounted for half of the world's industrial production (Sherry, 1995: 69). Despite Roosevelt's assertion that the United States would become the 'arsenal for democracy',

George Kennan rightly noted that the Alliance included a totalitarian state. Thus, the inclusion of the Soviet Union compromised the ideals of the Atlantic Charter and Roosevelt's Four Freedoms (Kennan, 1951: 66–7). British imperialism similarly challenged Roosevelt's ideas. These differences were the centre of historiographical controversy in the immediate post-war period as the Cold War further defined and polarised the interpretations of both powers' war aims.

However, it is also fundamentally important to remember the key differences between the United States and the European colonial powers – the Belgians, the Dutch, but principally the British and the French. Colonialism was an issue that Roosevelt loved to loathe; he was a fierce critic of it when given the opportunity. His ideological opposition flowed naturally with the cultural assumptions that linked the Declaration of Independence to the Monroe Doctrine through to Wilson's Fourteen Points. Ideologically, the United States stood for anti-colonialism and self-determination (despite its colonisation of vast tracts of the North American continent in the nineteenth century and its colonisation of the Philippines until 1946, and its neo-colonial relationships with many regimes around the Caribbean and Central America). Roosevelt raised the issue with national leaders throughout the war and indicated US support for post-war self-determination. He criticised colonialism with simple characterisations. He chastised French rule in Indochina, and of British colonialism he stated that it was 'the most horrible thing I have ever seen in my life. … The natives are five thousand years back of us. … The British have been there for two hundred years – for every dollar that the British have put into Gambia, they have taken out ten. It's just plain exploitation of those people. … Those people, of course, they are completely incapable of self-government' (Kimball, 1991: 129–45). He raised the issue with European leaders and especially with Churchill, but muted his opinion as the war progressed. Still, the language of the Atlantic Charter created a momentum and a context in which nationalist leaders could test US intentions. Washington was primarily interested in maintaining the cohesion of the Grand Alliance and if that meant compromising on issues of decolonisation, it was regarded as a short-term necessity. As Warren Kimball explains: 'Whatever his personal distaste for colonialism on moral and humanitarian grounds, his fear that it would disrupt any peace settlement motivated his wartime actions. But the requirements of alliance politics restricted his freedom of action' (Kimball, 1991: 128).

Although Roosevelt advanced his plans for a system of post-war Trusteeship, wherein the decolonised or liberated areas would be placed under the United Nations, Britain and France had no intention of giving up their imperial possessions. Charles de Gaulle and Winston Churchill, protecting the passing European system, joined together to resist Roosevelt's pressures. The struggle within the Grand Alliance of the 'Anglo-French ... against the United States over colonialism strained allied unity and forced Roosevelt, ever eager to avoid direct confrontation, to pursue postwar decolonization circumspectly' (Kimball, 1991: 129).

As the intentions of Article VII of the Lend-Lease Bill and point four of the Atlantic Charter indicate, US ambitions relating to decolonisation involved more than just promoting self-determination. Decolonisation afforded the United States the opportunity to gain access to the raw materials and resources of those areas closed-off by the European imperial systems. Following the 'lessons' of the 1930s, Washington did not want a return to the isolated economic systems that eventually led to economic depression and then to war. Washington's objectives included a multilateral economic system. Still, despite these ambitions and the compromises that Roosevelt made with Churchill and de Gaulle during the war,

> Rooseveltian idealism was not eclipsed by Rooseveltian realism. FDR was a standard-bearer of anti-colonialism even as he sought to secure the future of the United States' relations with Britain and France. He was already looking towards a new period in world history in which colonialism was an historical anachronism. (Orders, 2000: 79)

Thus the Grand Alliance united around the common purpose of defeating Hitler's Germany, but divisions between the United States and the Soviet Union on strategy and ideology tempered the cohesion, as did the divisions between the United States and Britain and France over colonialism. The prominent works on decolonisation and US strategy capture the US–European tensions in titles such as *Allies of a Kind* (Thorne, 1978) and *Ambiguous Partnership* (Hathaway, 1981).

Ambiguities lay at the heart of the Alliance strategy throughout. Negotiations on the 'Grand Strategy' in the early years of war took place in twos rather than as a combined effort of the 'big three': Churchill, Roosevelt and Stalin. It was agreed early at the *Arcadia* conference that a Europe first strategy should be adopted. Germany was considered the prime enemy that should be defeated prior to a concentration on Japan. Moreover, the Soviets, having signed an agreement with the Japanese, were more intent on bringing Britain and the United States into the war, opening up the second front in northern Europe. Until January 1943 strategic discussions created suspicion and some animosity because hitherto it was largely an Anglo-American discussion. The Soviets constantly pushed for the opening of the second front which, though promised earlier, did not actually take place until Operation Overlord brought the Anglo-American forces on to the coasts of Normandy in June 1944. Throughout the delay, the Soviets bore the brunt of German force, from Hitler's invasion in June 1941 to the turning point after the Battle of Stalingrad and the Soviet counter-offensives through the winter of 1942–43, which incurred millions of casualties. Not only were the arguments between the Soviets and the Western Allies acute, but disagreements between Washington and London also plagued the Grand Strategy. Churchill and Roosevelt opted for the 'peripheral' strategy that postponed the second front. Rather than relieving Soviet forces by engaging the Germans in northern Europe, British and Commonwealth forces advanced in French North Africa in late 1942, and the Americans launched their offensive in Italy in the summer of 1943, eventually securing British hegemony in the Mediterranean and access to the Middle East and South Asia through the Suez canal (Edmonds, 1991: 267–85).

In fact the resources used in Operation Torch precluded the option of the second front in 1943. General George Marshall objected to the plans on the grounds that the British had become nervous of directly confronting the Germans after 1940 and that the peripheral strategy dispersed forces too widely rather than using the US military preference for a concerted concentration of force. Roosevelt, however, overruled his military advisors for two reasons. First, he felt that some action was necessary in 1942 for political reasons, to demonstrate that the Soviets were not alone (Wood, 1987: 60–1), but secondly, because the peripheral strategy would incur fewer US casualties than the option of the second front.

More controversial is the suggestion that the North African option facilitated the projection of US power into the Mediterranean and allowed the two principal contenders for European hegemony, Germany and the Soviet Union, to exhaust themselves in the east prior to the concerted Anglo-American intervention in the west. As Operation Torch began in late 1942 and the invasion of Italy took place in 1943, the initiative diverted German forces in favour of the Soviets in the east. McCormick (1989) argues that the shift was now decisively westward, and it was a key question of how far the Soviets would or could advance. Torch meant that the US–British forces could not now enter the war through France till 1944. The key debates over strategy had a profound impact on the later origins of the Cold War, given the spheres of influence that were carved out through the Second World War. Washington avoided post-war political issues until its bargaining powers were increased through the implementation of Operation Overlord in June 1944. By that point US objectives differed from those of the British, who proposed a swift strike to capture Berlin as a symbolic victory. The United States instead opted for a more viable and rewarding strategy of capturing the Ruhr–Rhine economic core of Germany, ensuring Soviet dispossession and laying the groundwork for potential German industrial integration (McCormick, 1989: 37–8).

The narratives of the 'good war' and the 'Nuremburg consensus' need also to be offset against the US response to the Holocaust, especially after 1942, when the extent of Hitler's attempt to eliminate East European Jewry was fully realised. From the mid-1930s US media were reporting on the Nuremburg Laws, the burning of the Great Synagogue and *Kristallnacht* in 1938. Roosevelt initiated a conference to discuss the plight and destination of Jewish emigrants, but limited the numbers that the United States would accept during times of economic depression. As news of the concentration camps and the numbers deported to them reached Washington, Roosevelt withdrew the US ambassador from Berlin but did not break economic ties to Nazi Germany. Secretary of State Cordell Hull argued that economic interaction was essential to improving political relations. Stories of the camps appeared in the US media and by late 1942 Roosevelt confirmed that two million Jews had been killed. Washington did not increase its immigration quotas for European Jews considerably, nor did it attempt to bomb the camps or the railways, as suggested by the World Jewish Congress, to disrupt the slaughter. LaFeber posits four reasons for US inaction: Americans did not want large numbers of immigrants during a time of economic depression; the death camp stories were treated with suspicion in the wake of the propaganda generated in the First World War; top US officials were anti-Semitic and refused to deal with the immigration quotas in any meaningful sense; and the Jewish community was divided – the rescue of European Jewry might distract the State Department from its efforts to create a Jewish state in Palestine (Gilbert, 1981; LaFeber, 1989: 367–8).

PLANNING THE POST-WAR ORDER

Several roots of the Cold War lie in wartime planning for the post-war European order. There was a clash of visions between the US liberal internationalist optimism, British imperial strategies and the Soviet attempts to build a communist sphere of influence. While Washington attempted to promote a liberal economic system, there was considerable resistance from the British, who struggled to retain their colonies and their former world standing. The Soviets, too, advanced their communist agendas and spheres of influence in opposition to the US visions and the Americans' pursuit of their national interest. Compromises had to be made at the meetings of the 'Big Three' – Roosevelt, Churchill and Stalin – between 1943 and 1945.

The principal charge of compromise against Roosevelt following the Tehran Conference in late November 1943 was that he had sold out the Baltic States: he conceded that the Soviet Union could maintain control of Lithuania, Latvia and Estonia. Roosevelt was determined not to repeat Wilson's mistake of pursuing policies that were too idealistic, and he realised that compromise both in war and in the post-war order would be necessary to keep the Alliance together. From 1942 onward, Roosevelt increasingly opted for a 'spheres of influence' system rather than a universal one. His initial ideas of creating an Anglo-American police force to maintain post-war order shifted to include both the Soviets and the Chinese by 1942. Though the objectives were aimed at policing the various areas under universal principles, in practice everyone understood that this amounted to a 'sphere of influence' deal. Britain and the Soviet Union were not averse to the formula because they could maintain their separate spheres, in the colonial world and in Eastern Europe.

Both Britain and the Soviet Union were wary of the United States. In addition to the ideological differences, the Soviets were annoyed at the delayed opening of the western front and at their exclusion from the war in North Africa and Italy during 1942 and 1943. Britain too was increasingly wary of US attempts to pressure them on decolonisation. To that end, and to facilitate the spheres of influence agreement, Churchill and Stalin met in Moscow in October 1944, to defend themselves against what Lloyd Gardner has called 'American do-goodism or American imperialism' (1993: 196–202). Churchill and Stalin negotiated the westward shift of the Polish borders and what later became known as the 'percentages agreement'. The countries of south-eastern Europe were listed on a piece of paper and percentages indicating the relative control of either Britain or the Soviet Union were placed next to them. Significantly, US influence had been omitted. So, for instance, Britain obtained 90% control in Greece and the Soviets 10%, in Romania the reverse was imposed and in Yugoslavia and Hungary Churchill and Stalin split influence 50–50, and so forth. At the end of the meeting Churchill enquired whether it 'might be thought rather cynical if it seemed we had disposed of these issues, so fateful to millions of people, in such an offhand manner?' Though Roosevelt did not participate in the meeting, Washington thought the process would expedite further agreements.

Poland remained at the centre of the final meeting between Roosevelt, Churchill and Stalin held at Yalta, on the Crimean peninsula in February 1945. The 'Big Three' also negotiated the 'Declaration on Liberated Europe', which not only advanced the idea of a free and liberated Poland, but more generally asserted their desire to see the 'free elections of governments responsive to the will of the people' [*Doc. 17*].

Roosevelt placed US foreign policy in an invidious position. His rhetoric throughout 1944 led Americans, and especially the important Polish constituencies, to believe that elections would take place. Yet his diplomacy also left the Soviets with the clear impression that Eastern Europe fell within their sphere of influence. The language in the document signed at Yalta reflected the US ideals and the kind of rhetoric Roosevelt used in the 1944 electoral campaign. However, Roosevelt was principally concerned with maintaining the Alliance and realised that Soviet power was necessary for a stable post-war order; a sphere of influence deal could not be avoided. Soviet preponderance in these areas was the price paid for the delayed second front and the adoption of the peripheral strategy. As Soviet power was eventually consolidated and elections failed to materialise in Eastern Europe, Americans increasingly felt outraged and blamed Roosevelt for the situation. But as Leffler points out:

> The men who made US policy were anything but idealists. They cared little about human rights and personal freedoms inside the Soviet Union and the Soviet orbit. They were concerned with configurations of power in the international system and how these configurations affected US interests abroad and, more important, the American political economy at home. (Leffler, 1994: 49)

Given the importance of the Soviet military capacity, the rhetoric on elections appeased the domestic US constituencies even though Washington knew any elections would be fixed.

Beyond the political negotiations in July 1944 Washington and its principal ally, Great Britain, laid the cornerstone to the post-war economic system at Bretton Woods, New Hampshire. In an attempt to avoid the economic depression of the 1930s, Washington sought a more integrated and stable world economy. To do this they created the World Bank and the International Monetary Fund (IMF) and set an agenda for creating stable currency exchange rates and other mechanisms for an international liberal economic system. The US Under-Secretary of State, Dean Acheson, wanted

Such fears, misperceptions and wilful misrepresentations deepened the atmosphere of Cold War. Throughout 1946 attitudes hardened and compromise became increasingly difficult. By the end of the year the Soviets were pressurising Turkey on access and influence over the Dardanelles. In Greece, the British too claimed Soviet interference and the US aid mission to Greece reported on the possibility of the Soviets extending their influence into the Mediterranean either directly or through the use of insurgents. Most historians agree that the Soviets were not supplying the Greek insurgents and that the latter had limited ties to Moscow. It is an historic irony of vast proportions that Stalin had mostly kept to his percentage agreement with Churchill on Greece; it was Yugoslavia's Josep Broz Tito, the communist president, who was supplying the Greek insurgency. Nevertheless, the myth of a monolithic communism prevailed because within the mindset of official Washington, Truman believed that 'all communists took their orders from Moscow' (Paterson, 1995: 71).

On 21 February 1947 Britain informed Washington that it could no longer meet its commitments to the Greek government. Loy Henderson, the Director of the Division of Near Eastern Affairs, identified the importance of the message and the opportunity for Washington. After 150 years and two world wars, Britain was exhausted and the end of *Pax Britannica* was in sight. It was not only withdrawing from India and Burma, but also from Greece and Turkey. The new US Secretary of State, George Marshall, referred to the British 'abdication' from the region as having important consequences for its successor. Dean Acheson argued that should Greece fall to the insurgents this would not only have a psychological destabilising effect on the region, particularly on Turkey, but throughout Europe. US credibility was on the line. Within days President Truman engineered support in Congress for an aid package of $250 million for Greece and $150 million for Turkey. His alliance with Senator Vandenberg was crucial to the passage of the bill.

Vandenberg argued that Truman could not present his bill to Congress unless there were indications that it involved a Soviet threat. Moreover, the appeal had to be universal and avoid particulars; Washington could not be seen to be propping up a Greek monarchy. It had to be presented as a fight between democracy and communism. The bottom line was that if Truman wanted the money, they would have to 'scare hell' out of the American people (LaFeber, 1991: 53). Truman's speech of 12 March 1947 took up the conceptual imagery of Churchill's iron curtain, and drew another conceptual line across the continent, if not the world. His speech defined two ways of life and the necessity of making a choice at that moment in history. In the West there was freedom, elections and the will of the majority. And in the East there was terror and oppression, fixed elections, and the suppression of freedoms [*Doc. 20*].

US congressional committees reported extensive violations of civil liberties by the Greek government and that only about one-tenth of the insurgents were communists. Washington knew that the Greek insurgents were not receiving aid from the Soviet Union, that the Greek government was repressive and inept, but they were looking at the potential for the United States not only in Greece, but also throughout the Middle East. The Truman Doctrine acted as an announcement that the United States intended to extend its sphere of influence into the former British sphere in the East Mediterranean and into the Middle East (Cohen, 1993: 79).

THE MARSHALL PLAN: INTEGRATING EUROPE

While the Truman Doctrine extended US political interests, the Marshall Plan formed its economic counterpart. Though it was largely designed by and for West European politicians it could not be divorced from US Cold War strategy. Marshall decided to proceed with the European economic programme with or without the Soviet Union. At Harvard University on 5 June 1947 Marshall set out his economic programme arguing that it was not aimed against any particular country, but at alleviating 'hunger, poverty, desperation and chaos' and at reviving the 'working economy in the world' [*Doc. 21*]. Marshall's rhetoric provided the latitude for all Europeans to participate, given that Europe had not been explicitly divided, and that Washington did not want to appear as the instigators of the division; but it was clear to all that the plan was exclusively, if implicitly, designed to revive the economies of Western Europe. Internally, Kennan made it clear that aid would not be advanced to countries that did not open their economies to US exports. As he indicated, 'the Russian satellite countries would either exclude themselves by unwillingness to accept the proposed conditions or agree to abandon the exclusive orientation of their economies'. But the Soviets had made it clear that they intended to pursue exclusive five-year plans and their pressure on the 'satellites' in their sphere ensured that Eastern Europe would not participate in the Marshall Plan (Kennan, quoted in Crockatt, 1995: 78).

The economic situation in Britain, France, Italy and Germany was desperate. Productivity had reached pre-war levels by 1947, but there was a shortage of US dollars to purchase US goods. Moreover, inflation was high, distribution was poor, and visions of potential unrest and advances by the European left grew in the Washington mindset. Communism was perceived to thrive on fear, desperation and chaos, and so the plan was conceived in part to negate the appeal of the left. The British and the French were the first to accept the initiative. Their respective Foreign Ministers, Ernest Bevin and Georges Bidault, began discussions in Paris. Following pressure from the French Communist Party, the Soviets were extended an invitation. Soviet

Foreign Minister, Vyacheslav Molotov, arrived at the conference indicating a serious intention to consider the plan. His ultimate response was that each country should fashion its own plan and present it to Washington. But Britain and France, in line with US instructions, stressed that the plan had to be Europe-wide, integrating the economies of the continent. Molotov left the conference warning that the United States would undermine European sovereignty, that Germany would be revived and that the continent would be divided, creating new difficulties. Poland, Czechoslovakia, Hungary and Romania were still interested in participating, although ultimately Stalin pressurised them into withdrawing. A revived Germany, as the industrial powerhouse of Europe, was very much within Washington's plans. Molotov soon after initiated a plan for the East.

The remaining sixteen nations ultimately requested $28 billion over four years. Washington countered with an offer of $17 billion. The requests languished in the US Congress until the impetus for action was found after the Czech coup of February 1948 which got rid of the last non-communist government of Eastern Europe. Momentum increased in two weeks in March, assisted by Senator Vandenberg's rhetoric suggesting that the plan was a 'calculated risk' to 'help stop World War III before it starts. ... The Iron Curtain must not come to the rims of the Atlantic either by aggression or by default' (Ambrose, 1988: 90–1). On 15 March the US Senate endorsed the plan and the following day the Brussels Treaty was initiated. Truman initially received $5.3 billion for the European Recovery Plan (ERP), and eventually, between 1948 and 1952, spent $13 billion.

Though the US aims included a revived West European economy that could be integrated into the US economic sphere, much of the detailed planning was handed over to the Europeans themselves, whose own agendas therefore also had to be accommodated. The British resisted currency convertibility, which would drive down the reserves of sterling and jeopardise Prime Minister Clement Attlee's Labour welfare programmes. The French were particularly concerned about German remilitarisation. For the United States, the plan provided an economic side to containment, stimulated greater productivity, and mitigated the development of national capitalist programmes or ones that Europeans developed with their colonies at the exclusion of the United States. For Europeans, it served to bridge the dollar gap and contain Germany. Maier refers to the relationship as one of 'consensual hegemony' (Maier, 1994: 154–74). Or, to use Geir Lundestad's formulation, Washington created an 'empire by integration' (Lundestad, 1998a). The father of European integration, Jean Monnet, indicated that it was the first time in history that a great power 'instead of basing its policy on ruling by dividing, has consistently and resolutely backed the creation of a large Community, uniting peoples previously apart' (Lundestad, 1998a: 3). Washington wanted to keep the revived Europe within a wider Atlantic community, and at that point felt that such an economic plan was necessary, even though Europe was to become a third force in world politics later (Lundestad, 1996: 2–4 and 1998a: 29–39).

Within the 'community' each state was wary of the others' intentions. The Marshall Plan may not have so much as rescued European economies as ensured that they became integrated into the US economic system. The financial crisis of 1947 forced an abandonment of the US economic system crafted at Bretton Woods. The Marshall Plan was an attempt to reintegrate and revive the fortunes of the faltering vision. It was essentially a response to the 'dollar gap' and the European payments problem, which basically meant that Europeans did not possess enough dollars to trade effectively and integrate with the US economy. Between 1946 and 1947 the dollar gap increased from $8 billion to $12 billion. If the trend continued, European countries would be forced to trade within their economic spheres rather than across the Atlantic, as Washington desired. Without German productivity West Europeans did not have enough dollars to import US goods and keep that economy healthy. The ultimate US aim was to sweep away the European nation-state and integrate Europe into one economy and eventually a political union, firmly within an Atlantic setting. Yet European plans were different from those of Washington. The structures of European recovery were found in the European Payments Union and the European Coal and Steel Community. European ideas ultimately frustrated US ambitions and led them to pursue their own schemes of integration, rescuing their nation-states in the process (Milward, 1984: 462–74; McCormick, 1989: 73–80).

Despite some limitations on US ambitions, the results were still acceptable to Washington. It considered that the wealth generated would eliminate ideology from politics and reduce the appeal of the left in Europe. The economies were more or less integrated, unilateral capitalist growth had been averted, and US exports found homes in European economies. Such economic development and integration averted Soviet subversion or the appeal of the left and mobilised Europeans to support the post-war rearmament programmes. Cooperation among the corporate elite created 'an interdependent unit large enough to reconcile Germany's recovery with France's economic and military security'. Thus, the United States created an empire through collaboration (Hogan, 1987: 427–31, 443–4).

Though the Organisation for European Economic Cooperation (OEEC) was set up to handle the Marshall Aid and to promote further integration of trade, which increased rapidly, there was also a political and security dimension to integration. In the spring of 1948 the origins of the Council of Europe emerged through a conference of Europeans searching for further integration, especially in political and economic matters. Britain, of course, dragged its feet, worrying about limitations on its sovereignty, its 'special

BYSTANDERS: EASTERN EUROPE AND HUNGARY

Despite the universal rhetoric and ambitions of post-war US foreign policy there was little the Americans could do to assist the liberation of Eastern Europe without running the risk of initiating another world war with the Soviets. US efforts were largely limited to covert actions. Yet the Truman administration's Policy Planning Study (PPS) 13 recognised that 'the danger of war is vastly exaggerated in many quarters. The Soviet Government neither wants nor expects war with us in the foreseeable future' (PPS 13, 6 November 1947, in Etzold and Gaddis, 1978: 90–7). They realised too that the Soviets would protect their interests in Eastern Europe, especially after Tito's Yugoslavia challenged Soviet hegemony and was expelled from Comintern. In June 1948 President Truman authorised the use of covert operations throughout Eastern Europe. Such operations included '[p]ropaganda, economic warfare; preventative direct action, including sabotage, anti-sabotage, demolition and evacuation measures; subversion against hostile states, including assistance to underground resistance movements, guerrillas and refugee liberation groups, and support of indigenous anti-communist elements in threatened countries of the free world (Prados, 1986: 28–9).

Under President Dwight Eisenhower (1953–61) and Secretary of State John Foster Dulles there was little further action in terms of subversive covert operations, other than extensive propaganda (Lucas, 1999). Dulles talked about 'liberation' and rolling back the communist regimes of Eastern Europe. But when the opportunity arose, little was done.

Following Stalin's death and the threat of 'peaceful coexistence', the situation in Eastern Europe remained unpredictable. Riots broke out in East Berlin in 1953. There were clear messages from East European capitals that the Stalinist emphasis on development through heavy industry left people's living standards far below their expectations and far below the living standards of the West. By the time Khrushchev consolidated his power, at considerable risk, he pushed reforms forward by denouncing much, but not all, of what occurred during the Stalinist period. At the Twentieth Party Congress of the Soviet Union in February 1956, Khrushchev charged Stalin with the murder of party officials and the officer corps, which left the Soviet Union vulnerable. He argued that Stalin pursued misguided policies in industrial and agricultural development, he mishandled Tito's removal of Yugoslavia from the Soviet bloc, and laid out numerous other charges.

The reverberations around Eastern Europe were rapid. By April Cominform was dissolved, sending the signal that ideological conformity was no longer required. From here on in several different roads to socialism could be pursued; even various national forms of socialism might be tolerated. There was slightly more freedom in the Eastern bloc, but the bottom line was that they remained in the Warsaw Pact set up in May 1955. Khrushchev reaffirmed this message of greater freedom at a meeting with Tito in June 1956. Days later riots filled the streets of Poznan. The Poles demanded more freedom and more food. They brought about the end of collectivisation in agriculture and set up workers' councils in industry. But crucially, their new leader, Wladyslaw Gomulka, recently released from prison, ultimately convinced the Soviets that their reforms were limited and they did not intend to leave the Soviet bloc.

Hungarians were a bit more ambitious and therefore more threatening to Soviet hegemony in East Europe. Riots erupted in Budapest in June 1956. They were encouraged by the *Voice of America* and Radio Free Europe. Their demands were similar to those of the Poles, including a more liberal leadership. But while the Poles had made it clear that they would remain in Moscow's orbit, the Hungarians threatened to break out of the Soviet sphere. Since 1953 Hungarian Prime Minister Imré Nagy followed Malenkov in loosening economic controls. Further intellectual freedom allowed Hungarians to begin expressing desires for greater national independence along the lines Yugoslavia had followed. As Malenkov lost influence in Moscow, Nagy's plans were soon curtailed. He was replaced by Rakosi, whose hard-line response troubled the Kremlin. Hungarians insisted that Rakosi be replaced, only to get another pro-Soviet figure in Ernö Gerö. He differed little from Rakosi. Ultimately, the tension turned to revolution on 23 October 1956 when the Hungarian police fired on demonstrators. Gerö's request for Soviet military intervention discredited the Party and communism further. By 28 October Nagy had formed a new government with Janos Kádár, and by 31 October he had withdrawn Hungary from the Warsaw Pact and requested UN protection. Hungarian troops joined in the popular demands, and Moscow realised that such independent spirit threatened the stability of the entire region. The revolution was crushed. Washington was preoccupied with the Suez crisis, but the events also demonstrated the limits of US power and influence. The Cold War had clearly demarcated their sphere of influence, and their national interests dictated that beyond propaganda they could or should do little in Hungary or for East Europeans more generally. US and Western security concerns, not the promotion of their ideological beliefs, took precedence. The Soviets allowed some liberalisation, but to challenge the cohesion of the Eastern bloc, so soon after its inception, was intolerable.

TRANSATLANTIC DIVISION: SUEZ

The Suez crisis of October–November 1956 strained transatlantic relations considerably. The British and the French were the key US allies in Europe, but resisted taking a subordinate position to Washington for as long as possible. Washington accepted their global colonialism, secure in the knowledge that it was regressing over time. Similarly, Washington encouraged further European integration but wanted to keep it within the Atlantic framework. However, tensions erupted over US and then Anglo-French intervention in the Third World. The British and French governments had been quite critical of Washington's CIA, which overthrew the Arbenz government in Guatemala in 1954. The Eisenhower administration remembered that the British and French had argued that the case against Arbenz should be heard in the United Nations instead of at the Organisation of American States, which was dominated by US influence. Dulles instructed Ambassador Lodge at the UN, to 'let the British and the French know that if they take [an] independent line backing the Guatemalan move in this matter, it would mean we would feel entirely free without regard to their position in relation to any such matters as any of their colonial problems in Egypt, Cyprus ...' (G. Smith, 1994: 84). When the British and the French did take independent action in Egypt in 1956, the United States demonstrated that their independence was limited. The transatlantic relationship cannot be described as one of control, but in the case of the Suez crisis the allies were brought quickly into line (Brands, 1993: 58). Washington could not be seen to support such colonial-type action at the time when Third World nationalism was rising and nationalist support was crucial to securing US interests and strategic objectives in the Cold War.

British informal control over Egypt suffered following the coup that removed King Farouk in 1952, and eventually brought Colonel Gamal Abdel Nasser to power in 1954. By July 1956, as a result of Nasser's procurement of Czechoslovakian weapons and because the US Israeli lobby opposed the project, the United States withdrew funding for the construction of the Aswan Dam. Nasser immediately nationalised the Suez Canal Company, indicating that its tolls would be used to compensate for the financial loss. Apart from the immediate implications, Nasser's control of the canal also threatened the flow of goods and commodities, especially oil, to and from the European economy. By early November, British, French and Israeli forces invaded Egypt to reclaim control of the canal and attempted to undermine Nasser's pan-Arabism and anti-Israeli objectives. Nasser sunk ships in the Suez Canal, disrupting European supplies. Furious at not being consulted, Washington curtailed oil supplies from the Western Hemisphere, which exacerbated the European predicament, especially as winter approached (LaFeber, 1991: 188–9; Little, 1995: 479–84). Apart from the lack of consultation, Washington did not want to be regarded by Third World regimes as siding with European colonial powers. Moreover, with an imminent US election and the Soviet invasion of Hungary, Washington did not want to lose the propaganda opportunity that these events provided. Eisenhower blocked the British by selling sterling, undermining its value, and then blocking British access to IMF funds. The British withdrew in humiliation and months later Prime Minister Anthony Eden resigned.

The Suez crisis had a deep psychological impact on the British. They now understood that they could no longer exercise power independently if the United States opposed them. Eden's decision to invade with France and Israel was an attempt to act alone; it 'was a final attempt to establish that Britain did not require Washington's endorsement to defend her interests'. In this attempt to restore equality Britain paid the 'price of permanent subservience'. Washington's interests could not risk the potential destabilisation or alienation of other Middle Eastern regimes, especially Saudi Arabia (Lucas, 1991: 324–30).

The US interests were not that different from those of the British. The transatlantic crisis resulted more from the methods used and the timing of the Anglo-French intervention. Had they considered the US election and the Hungarian situation the outcome might have been quite different. Washington was not averse to covert action *per se*. The Americans had toppled Mossadeq from Iranian power in 1953 and Arbenz in 1954. Selwyn Lloyd's deathbed conversation with Dulles suggests that had different methods been used Washington's response may not have been so dramatic. Dulles asked Lloyd: 'Why did you stop? ... Why didn't you go through with it and get Nasser down?' Lloyd replied: 'Well, Foster, if you had so much as winked at us we might have gone on' (Yergin, 1991: 493; see also Lucas, 1991: 326–7).

Anglo-American hostility had not been so heated since the nineteenth century. By the end of November suggestions were made that Britain might withdraw from the United Nations and the Americans would be asked to leave their military bases in England. Ultimately, with the evacuation of British troops from Egypt, oil and finance became accessible, and when Prime Minister Harold Macmillan came to office in January 1957, relations improved considerably. A number of cooperative ventures were agreed upon in a series of meetings beginning in Bermuda in March 1957. Britain and the United States moved towards closer military and nuclear co-operation. The British accepted US intermediate-range ballistic missiles (IRBMs), and allowed US bases for early warning systems and submarines to be established in Britain. In return, the British were given greater access to US missile technology and ultimately Eisenhower and Macmillan agreed to the sale of US Skybolt missiles to Britain.

EUROPEAN UNITY

With the United States' role in the termination of the Suez crisis, and the humiliation of Britain and France, Konrad Adenauer remarked to the French Prime Minster, Guy Mollet: 'Europe will be your revenge.' A united Europe could slow the decline of the former great powers and maintain the influence of some key European leaders. European integration provided a process through which Washington's influence could be held at bay. Yet the European option and the Atlantic option were not mutually exclusive. There was a large degree of overlap, shared interests and values. Washington had worked hard to integrate with Europe since the Second World War. Still, considerable tensions remained among Europeans over the extent to which they should allow the United States to determine or influence events in Europe. As noted, Britain quickly mended its relations with the United States. It had more of a shared experience, it was not defeated in the war and was therefore more reluctant to give up on issues of sovereignty than its continental neighbours, who constantly worried about 'the German question'. Moreover, the British were not that dependent, relatively speaking, on trade with continental Europe, and pursued strategies that looked across the Atlantic and outward towards the Commonwealth (Reynolds, 2000: 128–30). For France, however, after their defeat at Dien Bien Phu in Indochina in 1954 and the increasing loss of empire, the prospect of a united Europe provided an opportunity to retain its place as a world power after Suez.

Throughout the 1950s Washington supported European unity. First Truman, then Eisenhower and Dulles realised that unity would be beneficial to the West. Under Truman it was important as a method of reconstruction, and later unity was seen as an essential part of Western economic strength that could withstand pressure from the East. But crucially, the US conception of a united Europe always lay within an Atlantic framework. It was considered an essential component of an overall Western alliance. Eisenhower referred to Europe as 'the third great force in the world', but the emphasis was always on Atlantic integration, most certainly in the military sphere, somewhat in the economic, and less so in political relations (Lundestad, 1998a: 54–5).

French politicians were likely to take a more independent line. National interests may not have diverged that much in the fundamentally important areas, but issues of sovereignty and prestige were still important. Washington had a tendency to lead without sufficient consultation, and often took Western Europeans for granted. While Americans thought of Europe as the 'third' force, Maurice Faure, a French delegate to the EEC negotiations, argued that it was a fiction to describe Britain and France as part of the Big Four: 'there are not four Great Powers, there are two: America and Russia.

There will be a third by the end of the century: China. It depends on you whether there will be a fourth: Europe' (Reynolds, 2000: 129).

There were several conceptions of 'Europe' at the time. The Soviets and Eastern Europe were bound together in Comecon. Western Europe, to use a well-worn phrase, was at 'sixes and sevens'. The Six – Belgium, the Netherlands, Luxembourg, France, the Federal Republic of Germany and Italy – were the initial states to form the European Economic Community through the Treaty of Rome in March 1957 [*Doc. 24*]. The productive successes of the European Coal and Steel Community (ECSC) prompted further negotiation towards greater integration. The three Benelux countries (Belgium, Luxembourg and the Netherlands) had already formed a customs union in 1948. The aim now was to extend that customs union to the members of the ECSC, and then to extend it further to cover all industrial and agricultural products. Led by Paul-Henri Spaak, the negotiations at Messina in 1955 resulted in a common tariff among the states. The eventual aim was to be in a position where Europe could compete with the United States.

The integration of the Six obviously did not include Britain, which caused some concern. Prime Minister Macmillan's external economic focus was more explicitly aimed at Atlanticism and the Commonwealth, thus the Six were constantly wary of London's other links. The long-term benefits of European and Atlantic integration outweighed the short-term costs of dealing with European economic tariffs, so Dulles supported the integration of the Six, in advance of dealing with the British. Hence Washington urged the Six to form the community before they entered into negotiations with the British, who might weaken the unity and therefore the utility of the Common Market. Washington assumed that the EEC member states could be influenced through the overarching structure of NATO, of which they were also members. And besides, few questioned US 'leadership' in the Cold War at that time. But the momentum of US support for integration was somewhat halted by the US balance of payments problem with the Six, unlike Britain. The support was further tempered in 1958 when Charles de Gaulle increasingly began to question US leadership (Lundestad, 1998a: 51–2).

The Seven – Britain, Sweden, Denmark, Norway, Portugal, Switzerland and Austria – in 1959 formed the European Free Trade Association (EFTA). EFTA removed trade barriers between the Seven, forming a loose economic group whose main connections were their various trade relationships with Britain. Since Washington had initially rebuffed Britain's Atlanticism, the grouping offered a modicum of defence against the integration of the Six. But trade with the other members of EFTA was of secondary concern. The United States, the Commonwealth and the Six were still more important. Macmillan worried about the tariff barriers that impeded British exports to

economic decline, Kennedy attempted to regain consensus in the Western Alliance. On 4 July 1962 he stated: 'the United States will be ready for a declaration of interdependence, that we will be prepared to discuss with a United Europe the ways and means of forming a concrete Atlantic partnership, a mutually beneficial partnership between the new union now emerging in Europe and the old American union founded here 173 years ago' [*Docs 26 and 27*]. Kennedy's Grand Design envisaged a Britain within the European Common Market, increased US exports resulting from the reduction of transatlantic tariff barriers, an attempt to place more of the defence burden on Europeans, especially in the area of conventional forces, and an attempt to control nuclear weapons through the Multilateral Force (MLF). Costigliola characterises the design as an attempt 'to bolster the American position by making Western Europe a unified, faithful helpmate' (Costigliola, 1984: 228, 250–1). De Gaulle was increasingly wary of Washington's suffocating embrace. He was outraged in the autumn of 1962 when Washington took unilateral decisions during the Cuban missile crisis, which in de Gaulle's view was an Alliance matter. He castigated Washington with the ironic statement, that he did not want to be annihilated without representation, recalling the colonial disgruntlement of pre-independent America. De Gaulle was further convinced that Britain was a US satellite after Washington scrapped the Skybolt deal in exchange for the Polaris missiles. In December 1962 de Gaulle met with Macmillan in an attempt to initiate a European missile system to replace the ditched Skybolt, though Washington had warned Macmillan against 'such an "unholy alliance"'. Macmillan soon obtained the sale of the Polaris to Britain from a reluctant Kennedy who wanted to phase out Britain's nuclear independence. In a disingenuous attempt to appease de Gaulle Kennedy then offered the Polaris to the French, knowing they did not have delivery systems for the missile. The French reaction was swift. Within the month, on 14 January 1963, de Gaulle's veto of the British entry to the Common Market signalled the loss of US hegemony in Europe and the failure of Kennedy's Grand Design. Within a week Adenauer and de Gaulle signed a friendship treaty. US nuclear policy during this period was directed at containing European independent initiatives. As Costigliola's succinct analysis demonstrates:

> The Kennedy Administration was shaken. The President became 'extremely concerned' over intelligence reports (later shown to be false) of a Franco-Russian deal to shut the United States out of Europe. Officials feared the strong-willed general might shape the Common Market into an autarchic bloc, closing out American business through discriminatory tariffs and investment policies. The nation's 'world leadership' appeared to be under attack. (1989: 27, 49–51)

Kennedy soon brought Dean Acheson back into planning discussions. Acheson indicated that the Germans needed to be reminded 'again the feel of our contempt'. Further, Adenauer should be reminded that US–German relations depended on the latter's commitment to NATO, the MLF, and British accession to the EEC. De Gaulle wanted to carve out a more independent role for a united Europe, with France at its centre. This necessitated British exclusion because it was considered too compliant to Washington's interests and de Gaulle worried that the EEC 'would be a colossal Atlantic Community dependent on America and directed by America, which would not take long to absorb this European Community' (Grosser, 1978: 200–1; see also McCormick, 1989: 131).

Washington favoured the British entry into the EEC as a way to get the Six to look across the Atlantic and move away from its more protectionist measures. Washington was also relieved that its support of the 1961 British application undercut the British ideas of taking all of EFTA into the EEC. The prospect of a protectionist Europe made up of thirteen states, without US leverage, was disturbing. It could hamper US trade and could truly become an independent 'third force' outside US hegemony. After Britain put in its applications the Under-Secretary of State, George Ball, told Kennedy that the neutral states in EFTA, Sweden and Switzerland, should not be able to weaken the Western bloc. Even though the problem of the neutrals was avoided, it was precisely because of the Anglo-American 'special relationship' that British entry and Kennedy's Grand Design failed (Dobson, 1995: 126–7).

DE GAULLE AND EUROPE FROM THE ATLANTIC TO THE URALS

Charles de Gaulle had seen off the immediate British Trojan Horse full of US power, but his ambitions were much wider. The Franco-German Treaty truly alarmed Washington, especially because of the form that it took. Washington had earlier supported the treaty, considering French–German *rapprochement* beneficial to the entire continent. But it was always assumed that it would be within the Atlantic framework and under the auspices of NATO. Washington warned West Germany that it might have to choose between France and the rest of Europe and the United States. Kennedy went so far as to remark that the treaty was an 'unfriendly act'. Suggestions were made that if Bonn persisted with such diplomacy, Berlin might not be protected indefinitely. The implications for German security were obvious. In February 1963 Kennedy pressed Adenauer to confirm that its allegiance belonged to the West. Adenauer's determination to maintain the treaty with France remained firm. But ultimately it was watered down by the preamble to the treaty, which indicated that Bonn had primary obligations to its 'multilateral treaties' rather than the bilateral agreement with France. Adenauer ultimately resigned in October 1963, replaced by the more US-friendly Ludwig Erhard (Lundestad, 1998a: 72–4).

Besides the Franco-German Treaty, de Gaulle struck out for a more independent Europe, outside the dominant relationship with the United States. He did not want to be in a relationship in which European allies were 'informed' rather than 'consulted' by Washington. He envisioned a Europe stretching from the Atlantic to the Urals and a more cohesive Six, with their CAP and Common External Tariff (CET) as key components in asserting independence from Washington. Further, by 1960, France exploded its first atomic bomb; it began to develop the *force de frappe* and argued for a more independent European deterrent capability.

In turn, Washington tried to limit de Gaulle's ambitions. The Dillon and then the Kennedy rounds of GATT were designed to undermine potential European independence in the economic sphere, while in the military sphere Washington proposed the development of the multilateral force (MLF) that envisaged greater European participation in the nuclear deterrent, albeit under NATO with a preponderant US voice. Moreover, Washington argued that Europeans could increase their share of the defence burden through larger contributions of conventional forces while Washington concentrated on its nuclear superiority.

De Gaulle sought more independence. He did not seek to withdraw from the alliance, but from the type of integration dominated by NATO and the United States. Washington promoted the idea of the MLF because it grew increasingly wary of the independent European nuclear capabilities. De Gaulle considered the MLF to be a US attempt to maintain its influence over Europe through Germany, now that its British option had been blocked in 1963. By 1964 de Gaulle worked hard to undermine the MLF and by November of that year Washington decided to move away from the idea.

De Gaulle remained a central concern to the Johnson administration's (1963–69) European policies. Though Washington was obviously preoccupied with the war in Vietnam, here again de Gaulle was seen as a disloyal member of the Alliance. He had called for the 'neutralisation' of Vietnam and then later of the entire region. He strongly objected to the war and argued that the costs of the war were being passed on to Europeans. The US dollar had been set against a certain value in gold, and as Johnson was determined to fight the war and build his 'Great Society' the only way he could pay for the two was to print dollars. The uneven value of the dollar in the United States and in Europe meant, in effect, that the Europeans were being taxed to help pay for the war. De Gaulle aggravated the situation by demanding gold from the United States, brought back by Air France, in exchange for the dollars. In 1965 he cashed in $300 million, demanding that gold replace the dollar as the international standard (Gardner, 1994: 266).

On 7 March 1966, de Gaulle took the most dramatic step in pulling France out of NATO's command structures and demanding that foreign forces be removed from French soil. Though the Johnson administration reacted calmly, internally it worried about the break-up of NATO and the possibility of a neutral France at the centre of Europe (Gardner, 1994: 274). The move was far more of a political act than one of significant military consequence. De Gaulle wanted to make the distinction between the Alliance, to which he remained loyal, and the organisation, which he saw as dominated by Washington. Thus he argued that France needed to adapt with the changing balance in the Atlantic relationship and 'regain on her whole territory the full exercise of her sovereignty ... diminished by the permanent presence of Allied military elements' (de Gaulle, in Grosser, 1978: 214). US forces were removed and the headquarters of NATO was moved from Paris to Brussels. Germany did not want to be forced into a position to choose between Paris and Washington, with the tremendous continental consequences that this involved. Within the year, after Britain submitted its second application to join the EEC, de Gaulle questioned Prime Minister Harold Wilson extensively on Britain's relationship with the United States on matters of defence and regional security. Within days of Britain's official candidacy, de Gaulle yet again vetoed British entry to the EEC, arguing that it would 'lead to the creation of an Atlantic zone which would deprive our continent of any real character' (Grosser, 1978: 217). Wilson later wrote that he had not passed the economic tests 'for entry to the anti-American, anti-liquidity gold club' (Grosser, 1978: 213–17).

Beyond the NATO issue de Gaulle searched for greater European independence. He insisted that European division and German division were European questions and should be settled by Europeans. From 1966 France initiated a period of *détente* with the East. In June 1966 de Gaulle made a high-profile visit to Moscow, and during the same period French Foreign Minister Couve de Murville visited Poland, Czechoslovakia, Romania, Hungary and Bulgaria. In the next couple of years de Gaulle visited Poland and Romania. His initiatives served as a precursor to the more widespread *détente* between the United States and the Soviet Union, but it is important to note that European *détente* with Moscow began before the US *détente* and lasted much longer. Indeed, when the Cold War returned in the late 1970s and early 1980s, many Europeans were reluctant to follow the route that Reagan's rhetoric led them (Garthoff, 1994a: 123–4).

Johnson initiated a policy of 'bridge-building' with Eastern Europe and the Soviets from 1966 to alleviate NATO's crisis and offset de Gaulle's manoeuvres. It was an attempt to move *détente* into the Atlantic framework. Dean Acheson even spoke of developing a 'good neighbor' policy towards the Warsaw Pact. Johnson's decision not to confront France and make *détente* a more attractive option if the United States was included infuriated Acheson. He admonished an advisor, after Johnson had distanced

CHAPTER SIX

US DECLINE AND EUROPEAN INTEGRATION, 1973–86

Given the US preoccupation with Vietnam during the late 1960s and early 1970s, Europe's place on Washington's agenda had slipped. By the end of the war the structures of the world economy and political relationships had changed. Politically, the world was no longer clearly divided into a bi-polar formulation. Europe, Japan and China increasingly asserted their power. *Détente* provided a period of relaxation for both superpowers to deal with their allies and to try to reassert their leadership. But the period was characterised by increased fragmentation and the world order moved towards greater multipolarity. As the European Community began to enlarge, Washington increasingly demanded that Europe not only accept more responsibility and a share of the defence burden, but also that US leadership prevailed. Because European *détente* with the East had been much deeper and broader, they were very reluctant to follow Washington into the renewed Cold War in the late 1970s and early 1980s. Clearly, with a greater European sense of independence and the US desire to maintain its leadership, the Atlantic framework continued to vie with the European ambitions.

DÉTENTE AND ECONOMIC TENSIONS

Three overlapping sets of events did not augur well for the transatlantic relationship in the early 1970s. *Détente* and the superpower relaxation of tensions created difficulties in the Atlantic Alliance, especially because Washington attempted to shape and direct the overall approach to the East. Following the war in Vietnam and the recurrent recessions in the United States, tensions loomed between an expanding EEC and America. The OPEC (Organisation for Petroleum Exporting Countries) crisis led to further animosity between Europeans and Washington. European enlargement from six to twelve and a renewal of the Cold War in the early 1980s demonstrated that their interests often diverged.

Though the superpowers continued their competition in the Third World, largely by proxy, both had to adjust to a more multipolar world during *détente*, which lasted roughly from 1968 to 1979. During this period the Soviets were challenged in Eastern Europe and de Gaulle and *Ostpolitik* in the West increasingly challenged the United States. Moreover, multipolarity in world affairs meant that apart from the US–Soviet competition, Europe, Japan and China became increasingly assertive. Washington considered its leadership of the Western world under threat and thought it imperative to maintain its interests and Western cohesion amidst the changes.

One element of *détente* was stimulated by the superpowers' *relative* economic decline: cooperation was imperative while they set their economies in order. The Cold War was too expensive at a time when alliances were in trouble. *Détente* provided some breathing space as Moscow and Washington adjusted to the assertions of power within their blocs. The centrifugal tendencies within the East and West, especially seen in the Sino-Soviet split of 1961 onwards, the Prague Spring of 1968, or de Gaulle's withdrawal from NATO, or Willy Brandt's *Ostpolitik*, threatened traditional assumptions on the alliances. The European challenges to the leadership of their respective superpowers was further augmented by the OPEC crisis in 1973 and the decision of Chilean citizens to elect a socialist government in the Western Hemisphere in 1970. By 1971 President Nixon reported to Congress: the world was 'at the end of an era. The post-war order of international relations, the configuration of power that emerged from the Second World War is gone. With it are gone the conditions which have determined the assumptions and practice of United States foreign policy since 1945' (quoted in Ryan, 1995: 105–7). The changes necessitated adjustment. Cohen suggests *détente* was like Washington 'asking the Soviets to contain themselves at a time when America's will to hold the line was in doubt' (Cohen, 1993: 183). Even though there was both cooperation and competition, the superpower relationship also encapsulated an 'element of mutuality'. *Détente* afforded each superpower the time and the space to deal with their respective economies and to deal with their respective alliances (Crockatt, 1995: 207).

During these shifts in the relationships the United States was passing through a period of relative economic decline. It had achieved a significant number of its post-war aims: the world economy was increasingly integrated, domestic prosperity had been mostly achieved, the Soviets had been contained, the European colonial order had passed, and many of the new independent economies were linked to the capitalist system. Washington now depended on the 'liberal international order'. Even though its relative position had declined, the 'global economic balances still left an environment which was not too hostile to its own open-market and capitalist traditions' (Kennedy, 1989: 562). Though not hostile, nevertheless, there remained plenty of competition.

Throughout the 1960s, US military spending, its overseas investments, and its trade deficit led to an unfavourable balance of payments, which pushed Europeans and the Japanese to cash their dollars in for gold and search for a new international monetary standard. Washington did not have sufficient financial leverage to influence the increasingly competitive economic blocs of the EEC and Japan, especially since in the 1970s the US experienced a series of recessions, 'that cumulatively constituted the greatest economic slow-down since the 1930s Great Depression' (McCormick, 1989: 162–3). In response, the United States first attempted to force the Europeans and the Japanese to re-value their currencies upwards. The Europeans complied, but not as extensively as Washington needed. The Japanese refused. The attempt to coerce the core economies of the Western world necessitated a change in the US position. The post-war economic system ended with Nixon's 'New Economic Policy' announced on 15 August 1971 [Doc. 28]. Washington unilaterally wound up the Bretton Woods system and ended the convertibility of $35 for one ounce of gold. The alternative was inconceivable. Washington could impose the same conditions that it had on Europeans through the Marshall Plan: it could deflate its economy, increase taxes, cut wages and impose job losses. However, the US was not willing to pay such a price. Although there was an attempt to restart the Bretton Woods system of convertibility in late 1971 with the Smithsonian Agreement, the dollar value continued to fluctuate. As Washington sought access to the East European and Chinese markets it realised that Soviet fears would have to be allayed. By 1975 Secretary of State Henry Kissinger described the advent of a new world order to the United Nations, emphasising the integration of the world economies (McCormick, 1989: 162–3, 167).

In essence there was a realignment of relations in an increasingly multipolar world. The United States moved closer to Eastern Europe and China, facilitated by closer political relations with the Soviet Union. West Europeans and Japan moved closer to the East and to Moscow, and increasingly acted independently of Washington's consent, and often in opposition to its interests. Under such circumstances the prospects of an enlarging and more independent European Economic Community somewhat alarmed Washington.

THE YEAR OF EUROPE AND EEC ENLARGEMENT

Kissinger and Nixon not only worried about *Ostpolitik* but also about the increasing cohesion and power of Western Europe. It was recognised as one of the five economic superpowers but the Nixon White House tended to downplay the importance of economic diplomacy, preferring to concentrate on the high politics of diplomatic and geo-political affairs. But their concerns about a more independent Europe continued throughout the period.

confirmed their membership of NATO, having joined in 1982 despite widespread public opposition.

RENEWED COLD WAR?

The Trilateral Commission, a group of government and business leaders from the United States, Europe and Japan, which was formed to coordinate policy after the Third World challenges posed by the oil crisis of 1973 and the subsequent attempts to negotiate a New International Economic Order (NIEO), provided key American personnel to the Carter administration (1977–81). President Carter chastised his predecessors for their concentration on the East–West rivalry at a time when Europe and Japan were becoming increasingly important actors. He attempted to focus more on North–South dimensions of world politics and emphasised human rights as the 'soul' of his foreign policy. In that vein he promoted closer relations with the EEC and made the first presidential visit to the European Commission in January 1978. Apart from this, Europe received little attention in US policy during Carter's tenure (Lundestad, 1998a: 109), and his attempt to move out of the East–West framework was ultimately unsuccessful.

The differences between Europe and the United States over regional crises in the Third World, the demise of *détente* and Europe's position on Palestine caused further friction in the late 1970s. As nationalist forces, sometimes backed by the Soviets, made gains in the Third World, and after the Soviets invaded Afghanistan, Washington initiated a military build-up, parts of which alienated Europeans, particularly the deployment of nuclear weapons in Europe. Europeans did not fully share Washington's fear of the Soviet Union and the new concerns with containment and rollback in regional crises; they did not want to see a return of the Cold War that prevailed in the final stages of the Carter administration and became even more stark under Reagan (1981–89). They continued with *détente* because their relations with the East were much deeper. The EEC further aggravated Washington in 1980 when it called for a Palestinian homeland, challenging Washington's pro-Israeli position.

Under Reagan the Cold War solidified. Defence budgets grew rapidly. His strategy was not that different from Carter's but there was more emphasis on defence. Reagan spent $1.6 trillion from 1981 to 1986 instead of the $1.2 billion planned by the Carter administration. Expenditures jumped from $206 billion in 1980 to $314 billion in 1990. By 1985 the Pentagon was spending $28 million every hour. They wanted a 600-ship navy, to be able to fight three and a half wars simultaneously and to gain the superiority to prevail in a nuclear conflict. When the administration launched the Strategic Defense Initiative (SDI) in 1983, Europeans thought they were more concerned with protecting themselves against Soviet intercontinental missiles than protecting the Europeans against the intermediate-range missiles. In European capitals there was widespread protest against Reagan's nuclear programme (Paterson and Clifford, 1995: 258; Galbraith, 1992: 126).

The Reagan administration wanted to negotiate with the Soviets from a position of strength and shunned talks in the early 1980s while it bolstered its military power. Reagan spurned the 'peace offensive' that Yuri Andropov offered Washington in 1982, an offer very similar to one later accepted at Reykjavik in 1986 (Walker, 1993: 272). US opinion and congressional reaction to the defence budget requests was ambivalent. They doubted whether the budget covering the years 1982–86, totalling $1.5 trillion, was strategically or militarily necessary or economically viable (Garthoff, 1994b: 33–42).

Remilitarisation was intended to project US power in the world again and to manage the economic recession by using the defence procurements to financially pump up the US economy. With the injection of finance into the faltering economy, the Reagan administration attempted to reverse the downward trend of US economic strength relative to that of its main competitors: West Germany and Japan. Over the long term, however, it meant that the United States was spending up to 8% of its GNP on 'defence', while the German and Japanese figures were much lower, 3.5% and 1% respectively, allowing them to invest more in the civilian sectors of their economies (McCormick, 1989: 216–19). The economy grew rapidly, but the benefits were short term. Between 1981 and 1985 the trade deficit grew from $30 billion to $130 billion, and the federal budget deficit grew from $59.6 billion to $202.8 billion over five years. SDI apparently justified a part of this vast spending, though critics suggested that if it were viable, it would create more instability because the European allies would not be protected by the system and, if the United States was immune from attack, Moscow would be tempted to unleash its weapons before they became impotent through the deployment of SDI (McCormick, 1989: 219, 227–30; Dumbrell, 1997: 66–7).

Reagan's military build-up exacerbated tensions with Western Europe. There was a fundamental problem in US strategy with the Western Alliance. Washington was in a quandary: as it continued to spend on defence, its economic competitiveness with Europeans, and especially with Germany, declined. Yet, if it wanted to maintain its leadership of the Western Alliance, the military sphere was one in which Washington was clearly in the lead. Altanticism and Europeanism vied with each other. While Europeans relied on the United States to protect their security, there were growing doubts about whether Washington would risk its own destruction to assist Europe in a time of need.

On the other hand, the separation of the blocs had become more apparent since the formation of the EEC in 1958 as Europe became a 'major manufacturing and trading bloc' which Washington regarded with increasing concern because it 'posed a threat to American interests' (Crockatt, 1995: 324). European agricultural policies dominated the transatlantic disputes during the 1970s. Washington found it had little influence on these economic issues, which were largely negotiated within the EEC. The tensions that characterised the Nixon period returned in the early 1980s. On security matters, Washington enjoyed greater influence because NATO was the main forum for discussions. Even though Washington initiated the military build-up in the late 1970s, it did not want to bear a disproportionate burden of spending on security while the Europeans remained economic competitors. Some leeway was expected, even though Europeans had no choice on the military build-up. Still, when the French revived the West European Union (WEU) in 1984 Washington worried about a 'European caucus in NATO' that may sap NATO's strength and cohesion (Crockatt, 1995: 324–6; Lundestad, 1998a: 111).

French Foreign Minister Claude Cheysson revived the WEU, which included Britain, West Germany, Italy, the Netherlands, Belgium and Luxembourg, because the increased superpower tensions in the Third World were affecting areas in which Europeans had former colonial connections. The WEU, unlike NATO, allowed the members to take coordinated 'out-of-area action'. The French were particularly critical of US intervention, from Nicaragua to Cambodia, and wanted to assert a more independent line. The WEU allowed for European action outside the NATO structure (Payne, 1991: 30).

The British were as usual out of line with their European neighbours. The relationship between Ronald Reagan and Margaret Thatcher was unusually intense and the United States and Britain formed a close alliance throughout much of the decade. Though it was strong, it was galvanised in 1982 when Washington ultimately decided to support its Atlantic ally against its hemispheric ally during the Falklands War. Other issues outside Europe on which London and Washington agreed made continental Europeans wary of British intentions, and whether the British would inhibit the depth and breadth of the EEC by remaining too close to Washington. There were, however, some hiccups in the 'special relationship', especially in October 1983 when Washington decided to invade Grenada, a member of the British Commonwealth. The ostensible (and incredible) reason for the invasion was to rescue US medical students who were in an increasingly threatening situation after a coup deposed Maurice Bishop. The invasion sent a signal to Cuba and Nicaragua about US resolve and capability. Yet the timing of the invasion was more likely prompted by the heavy loss of US life and credibility in Lebanon, shortly before. Thatcher was incensed at the invasion. She considered softening her position on the Soviet Union to upset

Washington and spoke on the BBC, condemning the violation of sovereignty by US forces (Dumbrell, 2001: 100–1). The relationship had moved a long way from 1982 when Reagan chose the British parliament to deliver one of his most famous speeches [*Doc. 32*]. Relations were repaired soon after, and by 1986 Thatcher was one of the few heads of government in Europe who supported Reagan's bombing of Libya in April that year. Washington requested the use of British air bases and imperiously imposed a deadline of less than twenty-four hours for a response. Though the British cabinet was wary, it ultimately concluded that British interests lay in better ties with Washington than the fear of reprisals against British embassies in the Middle East. The French and Spanish refused permission to use their air space and over-fly their territory. The US operation was wider than agreed, as they hit civilian targets and the French Embassy in Tripoli (Dumbrell, 2001: 102–3).

SOLIDARITY IN THE EAST OR WEST?

As Washington revived the Cold War atmosphere, the Soviet system was under increasing pressure. The economy had stagnated through the 1970s and come to a halt by the 1980s. The elderly Soviet leadership showed no signs of adjusting their stance in the Cold War to accommodate their internal problems. Yuri Andropov, and just over a year later Konstantin Chernenko, succeeded Leonid Brezhnev, following the latter's death in November 1982. Along with Soviet Foreign Minister Andrei Gromyko they took a tough stance on the West, opposing the military build-up and Reagan's deployment of missiles in Europe. As the tensions mounted between Washington and Moscow, the Europeans had the most to lose. Yet during the early 1980s Europeans on both sides of the iron curtain took an increasingly independent line within their alliances.

East European indebtedness and the second round of oil price rises in 1979 accelerated economic crisis across the region. The oil price and recession in the West meant a reduced market for Polish goods in the West and limited the intake of the hard currency Poland needed to repay its debts (Crockatt, 1995: 276). In Poland in particular, the rising costs of fuel and food led to widespread protest and civil disobedience organised by the trade union *Solidarity*. Poland was vitally important for Moscow. It not only acted as the traditional buffer against Western aggression, but also increasingly acted as an intermediary with the West and as a conduit for Soviet objectives in the Third World. But perhaps most importantly, its potential lack of allegiance to the Warsaw Pact would bring Soviet credibility into question, especially after the 1968 Brezhnev Doctrine. By August 1980, following widespread unrest in Gdansk, Polish workers gained the right to form free trade unions. Under the leadership of Lech Walesa, *Solidarity* appeared to offer an alternative political option. Membership grew rapidly, supported by

summit in Reykjavik, Iceland. From late 1986 Reagan desperately needed a foreign policy success. The Republicans lost control of the Senate in November, the Iran–Contra scandals engulfed the administration throughout 1987 and the October stock market crash undermined confidence. By December 1987 the Washington summit produced agreement on the INF process. Intermediate-range missiles began to be destroyed from June 1988. The summitry continued through 1988 without much substance, though Reagan and Gorbachev strolling through Red Square replaced the harsh images of the Cold War. When President George Bush (1989–93) was elected in November 1988, Gorbachev met with both Reagan and Bush in New York. Further unilateral steps were taken to diffuse the Cold War. At the United Nations in December 1988, Gorbachev announced that the Soviets would reduce their armed forces by 500,000, and withdraw several units stationed in Germany, Czechoslovakia and Hungary. Furthermore, 10,000 tanks would be demobilised. It was clear that Moscow was retreating from its traditional stance; Washington was forced to make adjustments.

REVOLUTION IN EASTERN EUROPE

Soviet power retracted in stages. From 1987 it began withdrawing from the Third World, most symbolically from Cuba in 1989. By late 1989 it let East Europeans determine their own fate, and by 1991 the Soviet Union dissolved.

When George Bush entered the White House in 1989 it made very little difference to Soviet priorities. Rather than maintaining the Soviet hold on Eastern Europe, Gorbachev sought more profitable relations with Western Europe, and further accommodation with Washington. Under 'new thinking', pragmatism, not ideology, was more important. Gorbachev and his advisors considered it more prudent to move away from the bipolar axis around Washington and Moscow to one aimed at Western Europe, centred on connections between Moscow, London, Bonn, Paris and Tokyo. The 'common European home' promised more profit during a period of decline. But such connections could also undermine the cohesion of NATO (LaFeber, 1991: 326).

On 4 June 1989, as Chinese authorities crushed the democracy movement in Tiananmen Square, the communists were routed in Polish elections. *Solidarity* won an overwhelming number of the seats that they were allowed to contest. After the Soviet interventions of 1953, 1956 and 1968 in Poland, Hungary and Czechoslovakia, and the internal crackdown on *Solidarity* in 1981, Soviet reaction was expected. But by this time Gorbachev had denounced the Brezhnev Doctrine and replaced it with the 'Sinatra doctrine', in which East Europeans could do it 'their way'. The Warsaw Pact released a communiqué in July 1989 stating there were no 'universal models of socialism'. After *Solidarity* came to power in June, Hungary opened its borders to Austria in July, and thousands of East Germans began to move to the West through various embassies. In October, when Gorbachev visited East Germany, it was ironic that the crowds looked to the leader of the Soviet Union for their liberation, and not to the United States. Eric Honecker briefly contemplated another Tiananmen in Leipzig, but subordinates refused to carry out the repression. Without an authoritarian crackdown or Soviet interference, crowds gathered across cities in East Europe. On 9 November, the Berlin Wall, one of the most potent symbols of the Cold War, was breached and then destroyed. The 'dominoes' continued to fall in Czechoslovakia, Bulgaria and Romania. Nikolai Ceauçescu resisted, but was soon deposed and executed. East European economies adopted Western economic systems, though within years, having felt the ravages of economic liberalism without the social safety-nets, they moved away from unfettered capitalist systems. The US economic response to the liberation of Eastern Europe was meagre. This time there was no equivalent to the Marshall Plan. What justification could the Bush administration have provided to Congress for the expenditure of billions of dollars? There was no longer a looming Soviet 'threat' to justify such expense. And besides, yet another sentiment of isolationism was running through some of the political debates at the time. Americans, backed by certain congressional leaders, were calling for a 'peace dividend'. They argued that it was time to redirect some of Washington's foreign expenditure towards the ills of the domestic economy and social infrastructure.

Of course the US rhetoric was somewhat triumphant, but Washington was careful not to gloat or provoke Moscow. On 12 December 1989, Secretary of State James Baker echoed both Churchill and Lincoln, recasting the Cold War within the assumed US traditions:

> From the Baltic to the Adriatic, an irresistible movement has gathered force – a movement of, by, and for the people. In their peaceful urgent magnitude, the peoples of Eastern Europe have held up a mirror to the West and have reflected the enduring power of our best values.

He indicated that the 'signposts' that had guided US foreign policy for decades had been lost. And with Gorbachev in Malta he stated: 'The world has clearly outgrown the clash between the superpowers that dominated world politics after World War II.'

Washington carefully considered its security and economic interests. Soon, negotiations on Moscow's entry into GATT were initiated. Six months later, in June 1990, the Washington summit aimed at destroying chemical weapons by 2002. The START negotiations were reinvigorated and negotiations on Conventional Forces in Europe (CFE) took off. By the Moscow summit of July 1991 Washington granted the Soviet Union 'most favoured nation' (MFN) status, which allowed equal access to US markets.

But beyond economic integration, Washington offered Eastern Europe comparatively little. Minor aid packages were negotiated but after Reagan's 1980s spending, their hands were tied by tight purse strings. Instead, Washington left the economic questions of the East largely to the European Community.

GERMAN UNIFICATION

One process Washington would not leave to either the Germans or the European Community (EC) was, of course, German unification. Washington supported German unification throughout the Cold War on the understanding that it would not occur within the context of a divided Europe. Washington did little to advance the process prior to 1990, though it was intimately concerned that West Germany was economically integrated into the EC and militarily integrated in NATO (Lundestad, 1998a: 142). But by the end of 1989 the European context had obviously changed dramatically and German unification was on the agenda. The speed with which unification proceeded took most by surprise. There had been no plans for unification in early 1989, but the collapse of the East German state, the tactics and political will of Chancellor Helmut Kohl and US backing pushed the process through within a year.

Kohl advanced a plan for state unity within five to ten years in November 1989. His logic for currency unification, which was pushed through in February 1990, was that if a standard value to the Deutschmark was not introduced, there would be a wave of refugees chasing the West German Deutschmark. Gorbachev indicated that it was up to the two Germanys to decide on their future destiny, though intermittently Moscow also made it clear that it would not like to see a united Germany in NATO. Within days the 2+4 formula was worked out, giving the Germanys the lead in the negotiations with the four post-war occupation powers: the United States, Britain, France and the Soviet Union. The currency union was rapidly brought into place in May 1990. The two central issues in the 2+4 process were the Polish borders and NATO. Kohl agreed that the Polish borders should not be renegotiated. As negotiations proceeded, Moscow provided that unification might depend on neutralisation, though this position was abandoned after Washington induced a change of heart in Moscow by signing a trade agreement in May (Reynolds, 2000: 562–4).

Washington insisted that Germany remain in NATO. Soviet troops were allowed to stay in East Germany until 1994, with Kohl assisting with both the costs of their presence and then their removal. Washington and Bonn moved with some speed to conclude an agreement before Gorbachev was ousted from power. Because Bush and Kohl thought his successors might not be as amenable to unification within NATO, Gorbachev's relative weakness within the Soviet Union gave him the opportunity to extract more concessions from Bonn and Washington. At the summit in late May and early June Washington drew up plans to assure the Soviets that a Germany in NATO would not harm their security. In effect, Washington maintained that Moscow would not necessarily become isolated, but that any objection to the NATO option might indeed lead to its isolation. Given the multitude of concerns that occupied Gorbachev and the various assurances received, Soviet objections to the NATO option were lifted (Clark, 2001: 90–4). Thus, Washington secured its continued influence with one of the Central Powers of Europe.

Thatcher and Mitterrand in Britain and France respectively were alarmed at the prospect of a united Germany at the heart of Europe. Since Reagan left office, the Thatcher–Bush relationship was not as close or as 'special'. Germany was increasingly the central concern for US diplomacy, as its economic potential and relative influence within the EC outweighed what Washington considered it could obtain through Britain. Indeed, Washington now referred to the Germans as 'partners in leadership'. Thus, apart from historical reasons, Thatcher and Mitterrand tried to ensure that the London–Paris axis was intact as the Washington–Bonn axis grew stronger. Thatcher, however, felt that ultimately she could not rely on Mitterrand, and he calculated that the Soviets would block unification, therefore he did not have to do anything. London and Paris quietly urged Moscow to slow the process, and even Bush, despite favouring it, worried about the speed with which it was proceeding. Consequently, Secretary of State Baker requested that East German officials slow it down. Bush supported a Germany 'whole and free', as long as it was within NATO and tied to the West through the EC. Further European integration once more provided the answers to the security concerns. The EC and NATO, the European and the Atlantic frameworks could shape the process (Reynolds, 2000: 565; Lundestad, 1998a: 144–5). By September 1990 the treaty of union was concluded. Kohl won elections in a unified Germany by the end of the year. With Germany unified, the Conference on Security and Cooperation in Europe (CSCE), comprising thirty-five countries, was able to declare the Cold War over in December 1990.

Nevertheless, despite positive political support, Washington worried about the potential German economic strength in the context of relative US decline. Following the costs of absorbing Eastern Germany, the Union would become a formidable economic power. Globally, Washington was intent on maintaining its central position and 'leadership'. In just over a year, secret plans revealed that Washington would oppose European competitors. A Pentagon Planning Paper indicated 'a substantial American presence in Europe and continued cohesion within the Western alliance remain vital'. Russia, after all, still remained a nuclear power. In the

Bosnia, Europeans accused Washington of ignoring Europe after the Cold War.

The strategy of selective engagement was problematic because it appeared as though the United States was either over-extended or that it lacked the will power. As the various propositions for intervention in Bosnia were debated, or the tactical opportunities of the 'lift and strike' policy (lifting sanctions on Bosnia and striking the Serbs) were considered, the importance of Bosnia to US interests were also debated. Pro-interventionists pointed to the humanitarian situation, the prospects of European instability or the possibility of wider regional conflict. US economic interdependence with Europe was vital to the US economy and instability would undermine US interests. A Clinton official compared the situation to the Gulf, where the interests were direct and 'the American people could understand', but in Bosnia the consequences were considered 'just as important, [but] they are less easy to describe'. Former Secretary of State James Baker indicated that it was one thing for the war to be fought within Bosnia, to be contained, but quite another should it threaten to expand: 'We have to make it clear that stability in Europe is the key. That should be the new NATO mission, whatever it takes, wherever it is. Because if we do get a wider Balkan war, we'll be back. Forget that reduction in US troops in Europe. We'd be back' (Baker, quoted in Ryan, 1995: 120–2). Ultimately, Washington did return with negotiations in August 1995, bombing in September, a cease-fire in October, the Dayton Agreement in November and US troops involvement in December. David Owen argued that a better deal could have been obtained in January 1993, had Clinton endorsed the Vance–Owen plan. The Dayton process was the only one Washington would accept, and it had to be American: 'Washington was unwilling to cede power to Europe as the guarantor of regional security' (Ignatieff, 1996: 8).

By 1998 Milošević again turned to Kosovo to shore up his domestic position. Military action and further ethnic cleansing were carried out against the dominant Albanian population who sought separation. Belgrade refused to grant Kosovo greater autonomy despite Western pressure. Bosnia had been contained within its borders, but in Kosovo there were speculations that the conflict might spill over into neighbouring Macedonia, with implications for Greek, and therefore EU, stability. From the early 1990s Washington realised that EU instability would require a US military response. The Bush administration sent a 'Christmas warning' to Milošević in late 1992: 'In the event of conflict in Kosovo caused by Serbian action, the United States will be prepared to employ military force against the Serbs in Kosovo and in Serbia proper.' The attitude was that Bosnia and Croatia could burn out, but Kosovo reached the geo-political limit with Europe. It was the 'red line' that could not be crossed, according to Clinton administration officials, and it would bring in NATO because of the threat to European stability (Danner, 1999: 10).

Negotiations were pursued through the Rambouillet process, though they were not exhausted. In essence, the West provided the Serbs with an ultimatum. Rambouillet also effectively called for free reign for NATO within Kosovo and the Federal Republic of Yugoslavia. After the Western deadline for compliance passed, United States and NATO credibility was on the line. The West was caught in its own ultimatum. Apparently London and Washington thought the operations would be over within days and Milošević would be back at the negotiating table. No contingency plans were made.

One day before NATO began its bombing campaign Milošević responded through the Serbian National Assembly. Military occupation was rejected, but he requested that the Organisation for Security and Cooperation in Europe (OSCE) facilitate a diplomatic solution 'toward the reaching of a political agreement on a wide-ranging autonomy for Kosovo and Metohija' and indicated a 'willing[ness] to review [the] size and character of international presence' (Chomsky, 1999b: 2). Though verification would be problematic, NATO did not investigate the possibilities.

NATO's response involved a bombing campaign that was disproportionate and exacerbated the immediate problems. The ethnic cleansing accelerated, as did the flood of refugees. Days after the bombing commenced on 27 March 1999, the American NATO Commanding Officer, General Wesley Clark, admitted that it was 'entirely predictable' that violence would intensify after the bombing. Clark soon indicated: 'The military authorities fully anticipated the vicious approach that Milosevic would adopt, as well as the terrible efficiency with which he would carry it out' (Chomsky, 1999a: 20–1). By 6 May the statement of the Group of Eight leading industrial powers did not differ that much from Milošević's 23 March resolution. With the threat of the introduction of ground troops, Milošević eventually withdrew his forces. The brutal Serb atrocities were evident in the unearthing of the mass graves throughout the region.

Ultimately, the Independent International Commission on Kosovo argued that the NATO campaign was neither a military success nor failure. Serbia was forced to withdraw its troops and police, and to sign an agreement closely resembling that proposed by Rambouillet. The systematic oppression of Kosovar Albanians was halted, but massive ethnic cleansing was not prevented. Moreover, the 'overall level of repression in Serbia increased' and Milošević stayed in power until he was deposed some time after (Independent International Commission on Kosovo, 2000: 5).

PART FIVE ASSESSMENT

DOCUMENT 1   THE DECLARATION OF INDEPENDENCE, 4 JULY 1776

Principally Thomas Jefferson drafted the US Declaration of Independence in June 1776. It set out the ideals of self-government and declared the thirteen states independent of the British.

When in the Course of human events, it becomes necessary for one people to dissolve the political bands which have connected them with another, and to assume among the Powers of the earth, the separate and equal station to which the Laws of Nature and of Nature's God entitle them, a decent respect to the opinions of mankind requires that they should declare the causes which impel them to the separation.

We hold these truths to be self-evident, that all men are created equal, that they are endowed by their Creator with certain unalienable Rights, that among these are Life, Liberty and the pursuit of Happiness. That to secure these rights, Governments are instituted among Men, deriving their just powers from the consent of the governed, That whenever any Form of Government becomes destructive of these ends, it is the Right of the people to alter or abolish it. ...

Extracted from Henry Steele Commager (ed.) (1963) *Documents of American History* (New York: Appleton Century Crofts), vol. 1, p. 100.

DOCUMENT 2   PRESIDENT WASHINGTON'S FAREWELL ADDRESS, 17 SEPTEMBER 1796

Washington was primarily concerned with ruling himself out as a presidential candidate in the future. However, the influential sections below outline the reluctance of the United States to become engaged in entangling alliances and is often cited to bolster isolationist arguments.

The great rule of conduct for us in regard to foreign nations is, in extending our commercial relations to have with them as little political connection as possible. So far as we have already formed engagements let them be fulfilled with perfect good faith. Here let us stop.

Europe has a set of primary interests which to us have none or a very remote relation. Hence she must be engaged in frequent controversies, the causes of which are essentially foreign to our concerns. Hence, therefore, it must be unwise in us to implicate ourselves by artificial ties in the ordinary vicissitudes of her politics or the ordinary combinations and collusions of her friendships or enmities.

Our detached and distant situation invites and enables us to pursue a different course. If we remain one people, under an efficient government, the period is not far off when we may defy material injury from external annoyance; when we may take such an attitude as will cause the neutrality we may at any time resolve upon to be scrupulously respected; when belligerent nations, under the impossibility of making acquisitions upon us, will not lightly hazard the giving us provocation; when we may choose peace or war, as our interest, guided by justice, shall counsel.

Why forgoe the advantages of so peculiar a situation? Why quit our own stand upon foreign ground? Why, by interweaving our destiny with that of any part of Europe, entangle our peace and prosperity in the toils of European ambition, rivalship, interest, humor, or caprice?

It is our true policy to steer clear of permanent alliances with any portion of the foreign world, so far, I mean, as we are now at liberty to do it; for let me not be understood as capable of patronising infidelity to existing engagements. ...

Taking care always to keep ourselves by suitable establishments on a respectable defensive posture, we may safely trust to temporary alliances for extraordinary emergencies.

Harmony, liberal intercourse with all nations are recommended by policy, humanity, and interest. But even our commercial policy should hold an equal and impartial hand, neither seeking nor granting exclusive favors or preferences. ...

> Extracted from Henry Steele Commager (ed.) (1963) *Documents of American History*
> (New York: Appleton Century Crofts), vol. 1, pp. 169–75.

DOCUMENT 3   THE MONROE DOCTRINE, 2 DECEMBER 1823

President Monroe's speech, later known as his doctrine has been described as a diplomatic declaration of independence. It sets out the case for a separation of spheres between the United States and Europe.

... [T]hat the American continents, by the free and independent condition which they have assumed and maintain, are henceforth not to be considered as subjects for future colonization by any European powers. ...

The citizens of the United States cherish sentiments the most friendly in favor of the liberty and happiness of their fellow-men on that side of the Atlantic. In the wars of the European powers in matters relating to themselves we have never taken any part, nor does it comport with our policy so to do. It is only when our rights are invaded or seriously menaced that we resent injuries or make preparation for our defense. ...

We owe it, therefore, to candor and to the amicable relations existing between the United States and those powers to declare that we should consider any attempt on their part to extend their system to any portion of this hemisphere as dangerous to our peace and safety. ...

Extracted from Henry Steele Commager (ed.) (1963) *Documents of American History*
(New York: Appleton Century Crofts), vol. 1, pp. 235–7.

DOCUMENT 4   THE OPEN DOOR NOTES, 6 SEPTEMBER 1899 AND 3 JULY 1900

The Open Door notes were principally advanced to various European powers to prevent them carving up China into colonies as Africa had been and maintaining the US ability to trade in the region.

... Earnestly desirious to remove any cause of irritation and to insure at the same time to the commerce of all nations in China the undoubted benefits which should accrue from a formal recognition by the various powers claiming 'spheres of interest' that they shall enjoy perfect equality of treatment for their commerce and navigation within such 'spheres,' the Government of the United States would be pleased to see His German Majesty's Government give formal assurances and lend its cooperation in securing like assurances from the other interested powers that each within its respective sphere of whatever influence –

... preserve Chinese territorial and administrative entity, protect all rights guaranteed to friendly powers by treaty and international law, and safeguard for the world the principle of equal and impartial trade with all parts of the Chinese Empire. ...

Extracted from Henry Steele Commager (ed.) (1963) *Documents of American History*
(New York: Appleton Century Crofts), vol. 2, pp. 9–11.

DOCUMENT 5   PRESIDENT ROOSEVELT'S COROLLARY, 6 DECEMBER 1904

The Roosevelt Corollary was advanced in part to prevent European powers from moving into the Western Hemisphere to collect debts or maintain order. Instead the United States indicated that it would be responsible for the maintenance of order and the exercise of a regional police power.

If a nation shows that it knows how to act with reasonable efficiency and decency in social and political matters, if it keeps order and pays its obligations, it need fear no interference from the United States. Chronic wrongdoing, or an impotence which results in general loosening of the ties of civilized society, may in America, as elsewhere, ultimately require intervention by some civilized nation, and in the Western Hemisphere the

meager enough results, indeed, after all was accomplished that could be accomplished, but always with a clear view, at least, of what the heart and conscience of mankind demanded. ... Property can be paid for; the lives of peaceful and innocent people cannot be. The present German submarine warfare against commerce is a warfare against mankind. It is a war against all nations. American ships have been sunk, American lives taken in ways which it has stirred us very deeply to learn of; but the ships and people of other neutral and friendly nations have been sunk and overwhelmed in the waters in the same way. There has been no discrimination. The challenge is to all mankind. Each nation must decide for itself how it will meet it. ... Our motive will not be revenge or the victorious assertion of the physical might of the nation, but only the vindication of right, of human right, of which we are only a single champion. ...

Our object now, as then, is to vindicate the principles of peace and justice in the life of the world as against selfish and autocratic power and to set up among the really free and self-governed peoples of the world such a concert of purpose and of action as will henceforth ensure the observance of those principles. Neutrality is no longer feasible or desirable where the peace of the world is involved and the freedom of its peoples, and the menace to that peace and freedom lies in the existence of autocratic governments backed by organized force which is controlled wholly by their will, not by the will of their people. ...

We have no quarrel with the German people. We have no feeling toward them but one of sympathy and friendship. It was not upon their impulse that their government acted in entering this war. It was not with their previous knowledge or approval. ...

... We are glad, now that we see the facts with no veil of false pretense about them, to fight thus for the ultimate peace of the world and for the liberation of its peoples, the German peoples included: for the rights of nations great and small and the privilege of men everywhere to choose their way of life and of obedience. The world must be made safe for democracy. Its peace must be planted upon the tested foundations of political liberty. We have no selfish ends to serve. We desire no conquest, no dominion. We seek no indemnities for ourselves, no material compensation for the sacrifices we shall freely make. We are but one of the champions of the rights of mankind. We shall be satisfied when those rights have been made as secure as the faith and the freedom of nations can make them. ...

Extracted from Henry Steele Commager (ed.) (1963) *Documents of American History*
(New York: Appleton Century Crofts), vol. 2, pp. 128–32.

DOCUMENT 9   WILSON TO CONGRESS: THE FOURTEEN POINTS, 8 JANUARY 1918

The Fourteen Points were advanced as the basis on which negotiations could begin and the basis for the German surrender. They also set out key US ambitions for the post-war period containing key ideas that would return in future US diplomacy and rhetoric. European leaders and US senators largely rejected the content of the points.

... It will be our wish and purpose that the processes of peace, when they are begun, shall be absolutely open and that they shall involve and permit henceforth no secret understandings of any kind. The day of conquest and aggrandizement is gone by; so is also the day of secret covenants entered into in the interest of particular governments and likely at some unlooked-for moment to upset the peace of the world. It is this happy fact, now clear to the view of every public man whose thoughts do not still linger in an age that is dead and gone, which makes it possible for every nation whose purposes are consistent with justice and the peace of the world to avow nor or at any other time the objects it has in view.

We entered this war because violations of right had occurred which touched us to the quick and made the life of our own people impossible unless they were corrected and the world secure once for all against their recurrence. What we demand in this war, therefore, is nothing peculiar to ourselves. It is that the world be made fit and safe to live in; and particularly that it be made safe for every peace-loving nation which, like our own, wishes to live its own life, determine its own institutions, be assured of justice and fair dealing by the other peoples of the world as against force and selfish aggression. All the peoples of the world are in effect partners in this interest, and for our own part we see very clearly that unless justice be done to others it will not be done to us. The program of the world's peace, therefore, is our program; and that program, the only possible program, as we see it, is this:

1. Open covenants of peace, openly arrived at, after which there shall be no private international understandings of any kind but diplomacy shall proceed always frankly and in the public view.

2. Absolute freedom of navigation upon the seas, outside territorial waters, alike in peace and in war, except as the seas may be closed in whole or in part by international action for the enforcement of international covenants.

3. The removal, so far as possible, of all economic barriers and the establishment of an equality of trade conditions among all the nations consenting to the peace and associating themselves for its maintenance.

4.   Adequate guarantees given and taken that national armaments will be reduced to the lowest point consistent with domestic safety.

5.   A free, open-minded, and absolutely impartial adjustment of all colonial claims, based upon a strict observance of the principle that in determining all such questions of sovereignty the interests of the populations concerned must have equal weight with the equitable claims of the government whose title is to be determined. ...

14.   A general association of nations must be formed under specific covenants for the purpose of affording mutual guarantees of political independence and territorial integrity to great and small states alike.

Extracted from Henry Steele Commager (ed.) (1963) *Documents of American History*
(New York: Appleton Century Crofts), vol. 2, pp. 137–9.

DOCUMENT 10   **JOHN MEYNARD KEYNES, *THE ECONOMIC CONSEQUENCES OF THE PEACE*, 1919**

The influential British economist Keynes outlined his reflections of the Versailles negotiations and the economic consequences resulting from them. In this section he describes Wilson's inability to keep pace with European tactics.

... When President Wilson left Washington he enjoyed a prestige and a moral influence throughout the world unequalled in history. His bold and measured words carried to the peoples of Europe above and beyond the voices of their own politicians. The enemy peoples trusted him to carry out the compact he had made with them; and the Allied peoples acknowledged him not as a victor only but almost as a prophet. In addition to this moral influence the realities of power were in his hands. The American armies were at the height of their numbers, discipline, and equipment. Europe was in complete dependence on the food supplies of the United States; and financially she was even more absolutely at their mercy. Europe not only already owed the United States more than she could pay; but only a large measure of further assistance could save her from starvation and bankruptcy. Never had a philosopher held such weapons wherewith to bind the princes of this world. How the crowds of the European capitals pressed about the carriage of the President! With what curiosity, anxiety, and hope we sought a glimpse of the features and bearing of the man of destiny who, coming from the West, was to bring healing to the wounds of the ancient parent of his civilisation and lay for us the foundations of the future. The disillusion was so complete, that some of those who had trusted most hardly dared speak of it. Could it be true? they asked of those who returned from Paris. Was the treaty really as bad as it seemed? What had happened to the President? What weakness or what misfortune had led to so extra-ordinary, so unlooked-for a betrayal? Yet the causes were very ordinary and human. The President was not a hero or a prophet; he was not even a philosopher; but a generously intentioned man, with many of the weaknesses of other human beings, and lacking that dominating intellectual equipment which would have been necessary to cope with the subtle and dangerous spellbinders whom a tremendous clash of forces and person-alities had brought to the top as triumphant masters in the swift game of give and take, face to face in council – a game of which he had no experience at all.

... Never could a man have stepped into the parlour a more perfect and predestined victim to the finished accomplishments of the Prime Minister. The Old World was tough in wickedness anyhow; the Old World's heart of stone might blunt the sharpest blade of the bravest knight-errant. But this blind and deaf Don Quixote was entering a cavern where the swift and glittering blade was in the hands of the adversary. ...

... He could have preached a sermon on any of them or have addressed a stately prayer to the Almighty for their fulfilment; but he could not frame their concrete application to the actual state of Europe. He not only had no proposals in detail, but he was in many respects, perhaps inevitably, ill-informed as to European conditions. And not only was he ill-informed – that was true of Mr Lloyd George also – but his mind was slow and unadaptable. The President's slowness amongst the Europeans was note-worthy. He could not, all in a minute, take in what the rest were saying, size up the situation with a glance, frame a reply, and meet the case by a slight change of ground; and he was liable, therefore, to defeat by the mere swiftness, apprehension, and agility of a Lloyd George. There can seldom have been a statesman of the first rank more incompetent than the President in the agilities of the council chamber.

From John Meynard Keynes (1920) *The Economic Consequences of the Peace* (London: Macmillan). From website: Vincent Ferraro, Mount Holyoke College, 103 Skinner Hall, Mount Holyoke College, South Hadley, MA 01075 USA (413) 538–2669. Fax (413) 538–2512, yferraro@mtholyoke.edu. See also Resources for the Study of International Relations and Foreign Policy: http://socserv2.socsci.mcmaster.ca/~econ/ugcm/3113/keynes/peace.htm

DOCUMENT 11   SENATOR HENRY CABOT LODGE OBJECTS TO THE LEAGUE OF NATIONS, 12 AUGUST 1919

Despite Wilson's tremendous popularity in Europe and European support for the creation of the League of Nations, Wilson was defeated at home. His delegation to Paris did not represent the US political spectrum and he

underestimated US opposition to the idea of collective security and the compromise of US 'unilateralism' that it entailed.

The independence of the United States is not only more precious to ourselves but to the world than any single possession. Look at the United States today. We have made mistakes in the past. We have had short-comings. We shall make mistakes in the future and fall short of our own best hopes. But none the less is there any country today on the face of the earth which can compare with this in ordered liberty, in peace, and in the largest freedom? I feel that I can say this without being accused of undue boastfulness, for it is the simple fact, and in making this treaty and taking on these obligations all that we do is in a spirit of unselfishness and in a desire for the good of mankind. But it is well to remember that we are dealing with nations every one of which has a direct individual interest to serve, and there is grave danger in an unshared idealism. Contrast the United States with any country on the face of the earth today and ask yourself whether the situation of the United States is not the best to be found. I will go as far as anyone in world service, but the first step to world service is the maintenance of the United States. ...

... The United States is the world's best hope, but if you fetter her in the interests and quarrels of other nations, if you tangle her in the intrigues of Europe, you will destroy her power for good and endanger her very existence. Leave her to march freely through the centuries to come as in the years that have gone. Strong, generous, and confident, she has nobly served mankind. Beware how you trifle with your marvelous inheritance, this great land of ordered liberty, for if we stumble and fall freedom and civilization everywhere will go down in ruin. ...

From PBS, Great American Speeches:
http://www.pbs.org/greatspeeches/timeline/h_cabot_s.html

DOCUMENT 12   THE NAVAL TREATY, 6 FEBRUARY 1922

Despite Wilson's defeat at the end of the war, his call for a general dis-armament was partially followed. During the 1920s the major powers agreed to limit the size of their navies. The agreement, however, only included certain classes of vessel and permitted growth in other classes.

The Contracting Powers agree to limit their respective naval armament as provided in the present treaty.

... Subject to the provisions of Article II, the Contracting Powers shall abandon their respective capital ship building programs, and no new capital ships shall be constructed or acquired by any of the Contracting Powers except replacement tonnage which may be constructed or acquired as specified in ...

... The total capital ship replacement tonnage of the Contracting Powers shall not exceed in standard displacement, for the United States 525 000 tons; for the British Empire 525 000 tons; for France 175 000 tons; for Italy 175 000 tons; for Japan 315 000 tons.

Extracted from Henry Steele Commager (ed.) (1963) *Documents of American History* (New York, Appleton Century Crofts), vol. 2, pp. 181–3.

DOCUMENT 13 THE KELLOGG–BRIAND TREATY, 27 AUGUST 1928

The US attempt to avoid a bilateral treaty with the French, who sought protection against possible future German aggression, resulted in a more general multilateral treaty, which renounced war as an instrument for the pursuit of national ambitions.

Deeply sensible of their solemn duty to promote the welfare of mankind; Persuaded that the time has come when a frank renunciation of war as an instrument of national policy should be made to the end that the peaceful and friendly relations now existing between their peoples may be perpetuated; Convinced that all changes in their relations with one another should be sought only by pacific means and be the result of a peaceful and orderly process, and that any signatory Power which shall hereafter seek to promote its national interests by resort to war should be denied the benefits furnished by this Treaty; Hopeful that, encouraged by their example, all the other nations of the world will join in this humane endeavor and by adhering to the present Treaty as soon as it comes into force bring their peoples within the scope of its beneficent provisions, thus uniting the civilized nations of the world in a common renunciation of war as an instrument of their national policy; Have decided to conclude a Treaty and for that purpose have appointed as their respective.

Article I: The High Contracting Parties solemnly declare in the names of their respective peoples that they condemn recourse to war for the solution of international controversies, and renounce it as an instrument of national policy in their relations with one another.

Article II: The High Contracting Parties agree that the settlement or solution of all disputes or conflicts of whatever nature or of whatever origin they may be, which may arise among them, shall never be sought except by pacific means.

Extracted from Henry Steele Commager (ed.) (1963) *Documents of American History* (New York: Appleton Century Crofts), vol. 2, pp. 221–2.

DOCUMENT 14   THE FIRST NEUTRALITY ACT, 31 AUGUST 1935

A Joint Resolution by the Houses of Congress, the Neutrality Acts, beginning in 1935, severely limited President Roosevelt's ability to engage in the war in Europe. During the late 1930s, despite US ambivalence towards the war in Europe, Roosevelt was increasingly able to compromise the various provisions of the acts.

Providing for the prohibition of the export of arms, ammunition, and implements of war to belligerent countries; the prohibition of the transportation of arms, ammunition, and implements of war by vessels of the United States for the use of belligerent states; for the registration and licensing of persons engaged in the business of manufacturing, exporting, or importing arms, ammunition, or implements of war; and restricting travel by American citizens on belligerent ships during war.

... Resolved by the Senate and House of Representatives of the United States of America in Congress assembled, That upon the outbreak or during the progress of war between, or among, two or more foreign states, the President shall proclaim such fact, and it shall thereafter be unlawful to export arms, ammunition, or implements of war from any place in the United States, or possessions of the United States, to any port of such belligerent states, or to any neutral port for transshipment to, or for the use of, a belligerent country.

... The President, by proclamation, shall definitely enumerate the arms, ammunition, or implements of war, the export of which is prohibited by this Act. The President may, from time to time, by proclamation, extend such embargo upon the export of arms, ammunition, or implements of war to other states as and when they may become involved in such war.

From website: Resources for the Study of International Relations and Foreign Policy:
http://www.mtholyoke.edu/acad/intrel/interwar/neutralityact.htm

DOCUMENT 15   PRESIDENT ROOSEVELT, THE FOUR FREEDOMS, 6 JANUARY 1941

The Four Freedoms provided the basis for the US ideological interests, parts of which found their way into subsequent US declarations and rhetoric.

... I use the word 'unprecedented', because at no previous time has American security been as seriously threatened from without as it is today. ...

... What I seek to convey is the historic truth that the United States as a nation has at all times maintained opposition to any attempt to lock us in behind an ancient Chinese wall while the procession of civilization went past. ... [W]e oppose enforced isolation for ourselves or for any part of the Americas.

... Every realist knows that the democratic way of life is at this moment being directly assailed in every part of the world – assailed either by arms, or by secret spreading of poisonous propaganda by those who seek to destroy unity and promote discord in nations still at peace. During sixteen months this assault has blotted out the whole pattern of democratic life in an appalling number of independent nations, great and small. The assailants are still on the march, threatening other nations, great and small.

... I find it necessary to report that the future and the safety of our country and of our democracy are overwhelmingly involved in events far beyond our borders.

... Our most useful and immediate role is to act as an arsenal for them as well as for ourselves. They do not need manpower. They do need billions of dollars worth of the weapons of defense. ...

Extracted from Henry Steele Commager (ed.) (1963) *Documents of American History*
(New York: Appleton Century Crofts), vol. 2, pp. 446–9.

DOCUMENT 16   THE ATLANTIC CHARTER, 14 AUGUST 1941

The Atlantic Charter is a key document of US diplomacy. Churchill and Roosevelt were the principal signatories, despite the objections of the former. It principally set out key US ambitions for the post-war world order.

[The United States and the United Kingdom] deem it right to make known certain common principles in the national policies of their respective countries on which they base their hopes for a better future for the world.

First, their countries seek no aggrandizement, territorial or other;

Second, they desire to see no territorial changes that do not accord with the freely expressed wishes of the peoples concerned;

Third, they respect the right of all peoples to choose the form of government under which they will live; and they wish to see sovereign rights and self-government restored to those who have been forcibly deprived of them;

Fourth, they will endeavor, with due respect for their existing obligations, to further the enjoyment by all States, great or small, victor or vanquished, of access, on equal terms, to the trade and to the raw materials of the world which are needed for their economic prosperity. ...

Extracted from Henry Steele Commager (ed.) (1963) *Documents of American History*
(New York: Appleton Century Crofts), vol. 2, p. 451.

DOCUMENT 17   THE 'DECLARATION ON LIBERATED EUROPE', YALTA CONFERENCE, FEBRUARY 1945

The Big Three, Roosevelt, Churchill and Stalin, met for the last time in the Crimea to discuss the post-war order, the occupation of Germany, the division of Europe and the United Nations. In addition they discussed the Declaration on Liberated Europe, which envisaged a democratic order.

The establishment of order in Europe and the rebuilding of national economic life must be achieved by processes which will enable the liberated peoples to destroy the last vestiges of nazism and fascism and to create democratic institutions of their own choice. This is a principle of the Atlantic Charter – the right of all peoples to choose the form of government under which they will live – the restoration of sovereign rights and self-government to those peoples who have been forcibly deprived of them by the aggressor nations.

Extracted from Henry Steele Commager (ed.) (1963) *Documents of American History* (New York: Appleton Century Crofts), vol. 2, pp. 487–93.

DOCUMENT 18   GEORGE KENNAN, THE LONG TELEGRAM, 22 FEBRUARY 1946

Kennan's telgram sent from Moscow to Washington became a key document of the Cold War, setting out the Soviet mindset and outlining the case for US response and 'leadership'.

... The USSR still lives in antagonistic 'capitalist encirclement' with which in the long run there can be no permanent peaceful coexistence. Capitalist world is beset with internal conflicts inherent in nature of capitalist society. These conflicts are insoluble by means of peaceful compromise. Greatest of them is that between England and US. ...

... Soviet efforts, and those of Russia's friends abroad, must be directed toward deepening and exploiting of differences and conflicts between capitalist powers. If these eventually deepen into an 'imperialist' war, this war must be turned into revolutionary upheavals within the various capitalist countries. ...

... Nevertheless, all these theses, however baseless and disproven, are being boldly put forward again today. What does this indicate? It indicates that the Soviet party line is not based on any objective analysis of the situation beyond Russia's borders; that it has, indeed, little to do with conditions outside of Russia; that it arises mainly from basic inner-Russian necessities which existed before recent war and exist today. ...

... At the bottom of the Kremlin's neurotic view of world affairs is traditional and instinctive Russian sense of insecurity. Originally, this was insecurity of a peaceful agricultural people trying to live on vast exposed plain in neighborhood of fierce nomadic peoples. To this was added, as Russia came into contact with economically advanced West, fear of more competent, more powerful, more highly organized societies in that area. ...

... In international economic matters, Soviet policy will really be dominated by pursuit of autarchy for Soviet Union and Soviet-dominated adjacent areas taken together. That, however, will be underlying policy. As far as official line is concerned, position is not yet clear. Soviet government has shown strange reticence since termination hostilities on subject foreign trade. If large-scale long-term credits should be forthcoming, the Soviet government may eventually again do lip service, as it did in 1930s, to desirability of building up international economic exchanges in general. Otherwise it is possible that Soviet foreign trade may be restricted largely to Soviet's own security sphere, including occupied areas in Germany, and that a cold official shoulder may be turned to principle of general economic collaboration among nations. ...

... It may be expected that the component parts of this far-flung apparatus will be utilized, in accordance with their individual suitability, as follows: To undermine general political and strategic potential of major Western powers. Efforts will be made in such countries to disrupt national self-confidence, to hamstring measures of national defense, to increase social and industrial unrest, to stimulate all forms of disunity. ...

... Everything possible will be done to set major Western powers against each other. Anti-British talk will be plugged among Americans, anti-American talk among British. Continentals, including Germans, will be taught to abhor both Anglo-Saxon powers. Where suspicions exist, they will be fanned; where not, ignited. ...

... In summary, we have here a political force committed fanatically to the belief that with US there can be no permanent modus vivendi, that it is desirable and necessary that the internal harmony of our society be disrupted, our traditional way of life be destroyed, the international authority of our state be broken, if Soviet power is to be secure.

... Gauged against Western world as a whole, Soviets are still by far the weaker force. Thus, their success will really depend on degree of cohesion, firmness, and vigor which Western world can muster. And this is factor which it is within our power to influence. ...

... We must formulate and put forward for other nations a much more positive and constructive picture of the sort of world we would like to see than we have put forward in the past. It is not enough to urge the people to develop political processes similar to our own. Many foreign peoples, in Europe at least, are tired and frightened by experiences of the past, and are less interested in abstract freedom than in security. They are seeking guidance rather than responsibilities. We should be better able than the Russians to give them this. And unless we do, the Russians certainly will.

From website: Resources for the Study of International Relations and Foreign Policy:
http://www.mtholyoke.edu/acad/intrel/longtel.html

DOCUMENT 19   CHURCHILL'S IRON CURTAIN SPEECH, 5 MARCH 1946

Churchill's famous speech delivered at Fulton, Missouri, publicly antici-pated the division of Europe, called for an Anglo-American partnership and was an early call to contain Soviet power.

The United States stands at this time at the pinnacle of world power. It is a solemn moment for the American Democracy. For with primacy in power is also joined an awe-inspiring accountability to the future. If you look around you, you must feel not only the sense of duty done but also you must feel anxiety lest you fall below the level of achievement. Opportunity is here now, clear and shining for both our countries. To reject it or ignore it or fritter it away will bring upon us all the long reproaches of the after-time. It is necessary that constancy of mind, persistency of purpose, and the grand simplicity of decision shall guide and rule the conduct of the English-speaking peoples in peace as they did in war. We must, and I believe we shall, prove ourselves equal to this severe requirement. ...

... A shadow has fallen upon the scenes so lately lighted by the Allied victory. Nobody knows what Soviet Russia and its Communist inter-national organization intends to do in the immediate future, or what are the limits, if any, to their expansive and proselytizing tendencies. I have a strong admiration and regard for the valiant Russian people and for my wartime comrade, Marshal Stalin. There is deep sympathy and goodwill in Britain – and I doubt not here also – towards the peoples of all the Russias and a resolve to persevere through many differences and rebuffs in establishing lasting friendships. We understand the Russian need to be secure on her western frontiers by the removal of all possibility of German aggression. We welcome Russia to her rightful place among the leading nations of the world. We welcome her flag upon the seas. Above all, we welcome constant, frequent and growing contacts between the Russian people and our own people on both sides of the Atlantic. It is my duty however, for I am sure you would wish me to state the facts as I see them to you, to place before you certain facts about the present position in Europe. From Stettin in the Baltic to Trieste in the Adriatic, an iron curtain has descended across the Continent. Behind that line lie all the capitals of the ancient states of

Central and Eastern Europe. Warsaw, Berlin, Prague, Vienna, Budapest, Belgrade, Bucharest and Sofia, all these famous cities and the populations around them lie in what I must call the Soviet sphere, and all are subject in one form or another, not only to Soviet influence but to a very high and, in many cases, increasing measure of control from Moscow. Athens alone – Greece with its immortal glories – is free to decide its future at an election under British, American and French observation. The Russian-dominated Polish Government has been encouraged to make enormous and wrongful inroads upon Germany, and mass expulsions of millions of Germans on a scale grievous and undreamed-of are now taking place. The Communist parties, which were very small in all these Eastern States of Europe, have been raised to pre-eminence and power far beyond their numbers and are seeking everywhere to obtain totalitarian control. Police governments are prevailing in nearly every case, and so far, except in Czechoslovakia, there is no true democracy.

From website: Resources for the Study of International Relations and Foreign Policy:
http://www.hpol.org/churchill/

DOCUMENT 20 THE TRUMAN DOCTRINE, 12 MARCH 1947

The so-called Truman Doctrine was delivered before a joint session of Congress with the intention of raising alarm about the exaggerated Soviet threat. Though specifically a request for aid to Greece and Turkey, the speech adopted universalistic language that divided the world into two conceptual spheres.

At the present moment in world history nearly every nation must choose between alternative ways of life. The choice is too often not a free one. One way of life is based upon the will of the majority, and is distinguished by free institutions, representative government, free elections, guarantees of individual liberty, freedom of speech and religion, and freedom from political oppression. The second way of life is based upon the will of a minority forcibly imposed upon the majority. It relies upon terror and oppression, a controlled press and radio, fixed elections, and the suppression of personal freedoms. I believe that it must be the policy of the United States to support free peoples who are resisting attempted subjugation by armed minorities or by outside pressures. I believe that we must assist free peoples to work out their own destinies in their own way. I believe that our help should be primarily through economic and financial aid which is essential to economic stability and orderly political processes. The world is not static, and the status quo is not sacred. But we cannot allow changes in the status quo in violation of the Charter of the United Nations by such methods as coercion, or by such subterfuges as political infiltration. In helping free and independent nations to maintain their freedom, the United States will be giving effect to the principles of the Charter of the United Nations.

Extracted from Henry Steele Commager (ed.) (1963) *Documents of American History*
(New York, Appleton Century Crofts), vol. 2, pp. 524–6.

DOCUMENT 21   THE MARSHALL PLAN, 5 JUNE 1947

Secretary of State George Marshall announced the US plan to provide Europeans with economic aid to address their difficulties and to provide them with the necessary dollars to import US products. The eventual European Recovery Programme helped European integration and enhanced Transatlantic ties.

In considering the requirements for the rehabilitation of Europe, the physical loss of life, the visible destruction of cities, factories, mines and railroads was correctly estimated but it has become obvious during recent months that this visible destruction was probably less serious than the dislocation of the entire fabric of European economy. For the past ten years conditions have been highly abnormal. The feverish preparation for war and the more feverish maintenance of the war effort engulfed all aspects of national economies. Machinery has fallen into disrepair or is entirely obsolete. Under the arbitrary and destructive Nazi rule, virtually every possible enterprise was geared into the German war machine. Long-standing commercial ties, private institutions, banks, insurance companies, and shipping companies disappeared, through loss of capital, absorption through nationalization, or by simple destruction. In many countries, confidence in the local currency has been severely shaken. The breakdown of the business structure of Europe during the war was complete. Recovery has been seriously retarded by the fact that two years after the close of hostilities a peace settlement with Germany and Austria has not been agreed upon. But even given a more prompt solution of these difficult problems the rehabilitation of the economic structure of Europe quite evidently will require a much longer time and greater effort than had been foreseen. ...

... The truth of the matter is that Europe's requirements for the next three or four years of foreign food and other essential products – principally from America – are so much greater than her present ability to pay that she must have substantial additional help or face economic, social, and political deterioration of a very grave character. ...

... Aside from the demoralizing effect on the world at large and the possibilities of disturbances arising as a result of the desperation of the people concerned, the consequences to the economy of the United States should be apparent to all. It is logical that the United States should do whatever it is able to do to assist in the return of normal economic health in the world, without which there can be no political stability and no assured peace. Our policy is directed not against any country or doctrine but against hunger, poverty, desperation and chaos. Its purpose should be the revival of a working economy in the world so as to permit the emergence of political and social conditions in which free institutions can exist. ...

... It is already evident that, before the United States Government can proceed much further in its efforts to alleviate the situation and help start the European world on its way to recovery, there must be some agreement among the countries of Europe as to the requirements of the situation and the part those countries themselves will take in order to give proper effect to whatever action might be undertaken by this Government. It would be neither fitting nor efficacious for this Government to undertake to draw up unilaterally a program designed to place Europe on its feet economically. This is the business of the Europeans. The initiative, I think, must come from Europe. The role of this country should consist of friendly aid in the drafting of a European program and of later support of such a program so far as it may be practical for us to do so. The program should be a joint one, agreed to by a number, if not all European nations.

Extracted from Henry Steele Commager (ed.) (1963) *Documents of American History* (New York, Appleton Century Crofts), vol. 2, pp. 531–2.

DOCUMENT 22   THE NORTH ATLANTIC TREATY, WASHINGTON, 4 APRIL 1949

Following the Berlin Crisis and building on European initiatives, the creation of NATO introduced a system of collective security across the Atlantic. Article 5 significantly required a joint response should any one of the member states be attacked.

The Parties to this Treaty reaffirm their faith in the purposes and principles of the Charter of the United Nations and their desire to live in peace with all peoples and all governments.

They are determined to safeguard the freedom, common heritage and civilisation of their peoples, founded on the principles of democracy, individual liberty and the rule of law. They seek to promote stability and well-being in the North Atlantic area. They are resolved to unite their efforts for collective defence and for the preservation of peace and security. They therefore agree to this North Atlantic Treaty:

Article 1: The Parties undertake, as set forth in the Charter of the United Nations, to settle any international dispute in which they may be involved by peaceful means in such a manner that international peace and security and justice are not endangered, and to refrain in their international relations from the threat or use of force in any manner inconsistent with the purposes of the United Nations.

Article 2: The Parties will contribute toward the further development of peaceful and friendly international relations by strengthening their free institutions, by bringing about a better understanding of the principles upon which these institutions are founded, and by promoting conditions of stability and well-being. They will seek to eliminate conflict in their international economic policies and will encourage economic collaboration between any or all of them.

Article 3: In order more effectively to achieve the objectives of this Treaty, the Parties, separately and jointly, by means of continuous and effective self-help and mutual aid, will maintain and develop their individual and collective capacity to resist armed attack.

Article 4: The Parties will consult together whenever, in the opinion of any of them, the territorial integrity, political independence or security of any of the Parties is threatened.

Article 5: The Parties agree that an armed attack against one or more of them in Europe or North America shall be considered an attack against them all and consequently they agree that, if such an armed attack occurs, each of them, in exercise of the right of individual or collective self-defence recognised by Article 51 of the Charter of the United Nations, will assist the Party or Parties so attacked by taking forthwith, individually and in concert with the other Parties, such action as it deems necessary, including the use of armed force, to restore and maintain the security of the North Atlantic area. Any such armed attack and all measures taken as a result thereof shall immediately be reported to the Security Council. Such measures shall be terminated when the Security Council has taken the measures necessary to restore and maintain international peace and security.

Extracted from Henry Steele Commager (ed.) (1963) *Documents of American History* (New York, Appleton Century Crofts), vol. 2, pp. 555–7.

DOCUMENT 23 NATIONAL SECURITY COUNCIL PAPER 68 (NSC-68), 14 APRIL 1950

NSC-68 has been described as the US blueprint for the Cold War. It acted as a call to arms for the United States, significantly increasing the defence budgets and accelerating the militarisation of containment. The language is stark and the document clearly outlined the fundamental differences between the United States and the Soviet Union.

BACKGROUND OF THE PRESENT CRISIS

Within the past thirty-five years the world has experienced two global wars of tremendous violence. It has witnessed two revolutions – the Russian and the Chinese – of extreme scope and intensity. It has also seen the collapse of five empires – the Ottoman, the Austro-Hungarian, German, Italian, and Japanese – and the drastic decline of two major imperial systems, the British and the French. During the span of one generation, the international distribution of power has been fundamentally altered. For several centuries it had proved impossible for any one nation to gain such preponderant strength that a coalition of other nations could not in time face it with greater strength. The international scene was marked by recurring periods of violence and war, but a system of sovereign and independent states was maintained, over which no state was able to achieve hegemony.

Two complex sets of factors have now basically altered this historic distribution of power. First, the defeat of Germany and Japan and the decline of the British and French Empires have interacted with the development of the United States and the Soviet Union in such a way that power increasingly gravitated to these two centers. Second, the Soviet Union, unlike previous aspirants to hegemony, is animated by a new fanatic faith, anti-thetical to our own, and seeks to impose its absolute authority over the rest of the world. ...

FUNDAMENTAL PURPOSE OF THE UNITED STATES

The fundamental purpose of the United States is laid down in the Preamble to the Constitution: '... to form a more perfect Union, establish justice, insure domestic Tranquility, provide for the common defence, promote the general Welfare, and secure the Blessings of Liberty to ourselves and our Posterity.' In essence, the fundamental purpose is to assure the integrity and vitality of our free society, which is founded upon the dignity and worth of the individual. ...

FUNDAMENTAL DESIGN OF THE KREMLIN

The fundamental design of those who control the Soviet Union and the international communist movement is to retain and solidify their absolute power, first in the Soviet Union and second in the areas now under their control. In the minds of the Soviet leaders, however, achievement of this design requires the dynamic extension of their authority and the ultimate elimination of any effective opposition to their authority. ...

THE UNDERLYING CONFLICT IN THE REALM OF IDEAS AND VALUES BETWEEN THE US PURPOSE AND THE KREMLIN DESIGN

The free society values the individual as an end in himself, requiring of him only that measure of self-discipline and self-restraint which make the rights of each individual compatible with the rights of every other individual. The freedom of the individual has as its counterpart, therefore, the negative responsibility of the individual not to exercise his freedom in ways inconsistent with the freedom of other individuals and the positive responsibility to make constructive use of his freedom in the building of a just society. From this idea of freedom with responsibility derives the marvelous diversity, the deep tolerance, the lawfulness of the free society. This is the explanation of the strength of free men. It constitutes the integrity and the vitality of a free and democratic system. The free society attempts to create and maintain an environment in which every individual has the opportunity to realize his creative powers. ... The idea of freedom is the most contagious idea in history, more contagious than the idea of submission to authority. For the breadth of freedom cannot be tolerated in a society which has come under the domination of an individual or group of individuals with a will to absolute power. ... The same compulsion which demands total power over all men within the Soviet state without a single exception, demands total power over all Communist Parties and all states under Soviet domination. Thus Stalin has said that the theory and tactics of Leninism as expounded by the Bolshevik party are mandatory for the proletarian parties of all countries. A true internationalist is defined as one who unhesitatingly upholds the position of the Soviet Union and in the satellite states true patriotism is love of the Soviet Union. By the same token the 'peace policy' of the Soviet Union, described at a Party Congress as 'a more advantageous form of fighting capitalism,' is a device to divide and immobilize the non-Communist world, and the peace the Soviet Union seeks is the peace of total conformity to Soviet policy. The antipathy of slavery to freedom explains the iron curtain, the isolation, the autarchy of the society whose end is absolute power. The existence and persistence of the idea of freedom is a permanent and continuous threat to the foundation of the slave society; and it therefore regards as intolerable the long continued existence of freedom in the world. What is new, what makes the continuing crisis, is the polarization of power which now inescapably confronts the slave society with the free.

The assault on free institutions is world-wide now, and in the context of the present polarization of power a defeat of free institutions anywhere is a defeat everywhere. The shock we sustained in the destruction of Czechoslovakia was not in the measure of Czechoslovakia's material importance to us. In a material sense, her capabilities were already at Soviet disposal. But when the integrity of Czechoslovak institutions was destroyed, it was in the intangible scale of values that we registered a loss more damaging than the material loss we had already suffered.

Thus unwillingly our free society finds itself mortally challenged by the Soviet system. No other value system is so wholly irreconcilable with ours, so implacable in its purpose to destroy ours, so capable of turning to its own uses the most dangerous and divisive trends in our own society, no other so skillfully and powerfully evokes the elements of irrationality in human nature everywhere, and no other has the support of a great and growing center of military power.

> From website: Resources for the Study of International Relations and Foreign Policy:
> http://www.mtholyoke.edu/acad/intrel/nscs-68/nsc68-1.htm

DOCUMENT 24 THE TREATY OF ROME, 25 MARCH 1957

The treaty established the European Community following intensified European negotiations during the 1950s. Washington politically supported the creation of the Community though also worried about the Community as a competitor to the US economy.

Determined to lay the foundations of an ever closer union among the peoples of Europe, Resolved to ensure the economic and social progress of their countries by common action to eliminate the barriers which divide Europe, Affirming as the essential objective of their efforts the constant improvement of the living and working conditions of their peoples, Recognising that the removal of existing obstacles calls for concerted action in order to guarantee steady expansion, balanced trade and fair competition, Anxious to strengthen the unity of their economies and to ensure their harmonious development by reducing the differences existing between the various regions and the backwardness of the less favoured regions, Desiring to contribute, by means of a common commercial policy, to the progressive abolition of restrictions on international trade, Intending to confirm the solidarity which binds Europe and the overseas countries and desiring to ensure the development of their prosperity, in accordance with the principles of the Charter of the United Nations, Resolved by thus pooling their resources to preserve and strengthen peace and liberty, and calling upon the other peoples of Europe who share their ideal to join in their efforts, Have decided to create a European Economic Community. ...

From Fletcher School of Law and Diplomacy, Tufts University
http://www.tufts.edu/departments/fletcher/multi/texts/BH343.txt

DOCUMENT 25   PRESIDENT KENNEDY ON THE BERLIN CRISIS, 25 JULY 1961

Berlin was at the centre of several crises during the Cold War. This time Kennedy had to respond to a Soviet proposal to end the shared control of Berlin and create a demilitarised city. Kennedy's response was categorical. The East Germans and Soviets soon erected the Berlin Wall.

Seven weeks ago tonight I returned from Europe to report on my meeting with Premier Khrushchev and the others. His grim warnings about the future of the world, his aide memoire on Berlin, his subsequent speeches and threats which he and his agents have launched, and the increase in the Soviet military budget that he has announced, have all prompted a series of decisions by the Administration and a series of consultations with the members of the NATO organization. In Berlin, as you recall, he intends to bring to an end, through a stroke of the pen, *first* our legal rights to be in West Berlin – and *secondly* our ability to make good on our commitment to the two million free people of that city. That we cannot permit.

We are clear about what must be done – and we intend to do it. I want to talk frankly with you tonight about the first steps that we shall take. These actions will require sacrifice on the part of many of our citizens. More will be required in the future. They will require, from all of us, courage and perseverance in the years to come. But if we and our allies act out of strength and unity of purpose – with calm determination and steady nerves – using restraint in our words as well as our weapons – I am hopeful that both peace and freedom will be sustained.

The immediate threat to free men is in West Berlin. But that isolated outpost is not an isolated problem. The threat is worldwide. Our effort must be equally wide and strong, and not be obsessed by any single manufactured crisis. We face a challenge in Berlin, but there is also a challenge in Southeast Asia, where the borders are less guarded, the enemy harder to find, and the dangers of communism less apparent to those who have so little. We face a challenge in our own hemisphere, and indeed wherever else the freedom of human beings is at stake.

Extracted from Henry Steele Commager (ed.) (1963) *Documents of American History* (New York, Appleton Century Crofts), vol. 2, pp. 706–9.

Kennedy's address outlined the emergence of a new Europe that had moved beyond merely a defence relationship with the United States. His references to the growing Atlantic Community belied the growing tensions between the spheres.

Finally, the united strength of the Atlantic Community has flourished in the last year under severe tests. NATO has increased both the number and the readiness of its air, ground, and naval units – both its nuclear and non-nuclear capabilities. Even greater efforts by all its members are still required. Nevertheless our unity of purpose and will has been, I believe, immeasurably strengthened.

The threat to the brave city of Berlin remains. In these last six months the Allies have made it unmistakably clear that our presence in Berlin, our free access thereto, and the freedom of two million West Berliners would not be surrendered either to force or through appeasement – and to maintain those rights and obligations, we are prepared to talk, when appropriate, and to fight, if necessary. Every member of NATO stands with us in a common commitment to preserve this symbol of free man's will to remain free.

I cannot now predict the course of future negotiations over Berlin. I can only say that we are sparing no honorable effort to find a peaceful and mutually acceptable resolution of this problem. I believe such a resolution can be found, and with it an improvement in our relations with the Soviet Union, if only the leaders in the Kremlin will recognize the basic rights and interests involved, and the interest of all mankind in peace. But the Atlantic Community is no longer concerned with purely military aims. As its common undertakings grow at an ever-increasing pace, we are, and increasingly will be, partners in aid, trade, defense, diplomacy, and monetary affairs.

The emergence of the new Europe is being matched by the emergence of new ties across the Atlantic. It is a matter of undramatic daily cooperation in hundreds of workaday tasks: of currencies kept in effective relation, of development loans meshed together, of standardized weapons, and concerted diplomatic positions. The Atlantic Community grows, not like a volcanic mountain, by one mighty explosion, but like a coral reef, from the accumulating activity of all.

Thus, we in the free world are moving steadily toward unity and cooperation, in the teeth of that old Bolshevik prophecy, and at the very time when extraordinary rumbles of discord can be heard across the Iron Curtain. It is not free societies which bear within them the seeds of inevitable disunity.

Copyrights: The copyright for all HTML sources is owned by the department of Alfa-Informatica of the University of Groningen (The Netherlands) and is protected by the copyright laws of the Netherlands, the United States and the Universal Copyright Convention. From Revolution to Reconstruction http://odur.let.rug.nl/~usa/p/jk35/speeches/jfk62.htm

DOCUMENT 27   KENNEDY'S GRAND DESIGN, PHILADELPHIA, 4 JULY 1962

As Europe increasingly asserted its growing power, Kennedy's Grand Design was in part an attempt to maintain the Atlantic framework over other possibilities and in part to maintain US leadership of the alliance. The speech on US Independence Day put forward a declaration of interdependence.

Thus, in a very real sense, you and I are the executors of the testament handed down by those who gathered in this historic hall 186 years ago today. For they gathered to affix their names to a document which was, above all else, a document not of rhetoric but of bold decision. It was, it is true, a document of protest – but protests had been made before. It set forth their grievances with eloquence – but such eloquence had been heard before. But what distinguished this paper from all the others was the final irrevocable decision that it took – to assert the independence of free States in place of colonies, and to commit to that goal their lives, their fortunes, and their sacred honor. ...

If there is a single issue that divides the world today, it is independence – the independence of Berlin or Laos or Viet-Nam; the longing for independence behind the Iron Curtain; the peaceful transition to independence in those newly emerging areas whose troubles some hope to exploit. ...

In most of the old colonial world, the struggle for independence is coming to an end. Even in areas behind the Curtain, that which Jefferson called 'the disease of liberty' still appears to be infectious. With the passing of ancient empires, today less than 2 percent of the world's population lives in territories officially termed 'dependent.' As this effort for independence, inspired by the American Declaration of Independence, now approaches a successful close, a great new effort – for interdependence – is transforming the world about us. And the spirit of that new effort is the same spirit which gave birth to the American Constitution.

That spirit is today most clearly seen across the Atlantic Ocean. The nations of Western Europe, long divided by feuds far more bitter than any which existed among the 13 colonies, are today joining together, seeking, as our forefathers sought, to find freedom in diversity and in unity, strength.

The United States looks on this vast new enterprise with hope and admiration. We do not regard a strong and united Europe as a rival but as a partner. To aid its progress has been the basic object of our foreign policy for 17 years. We believe that a united Europe will be capable of playing a greater role in the common defense, of responding more generously to the needs of poorer nations, of joining with the United States and others in lowering trade barriers, resolving problems of commerce, commodities, and currency, and developing coordinated policies in all economic, political, and diplomatic areas. We see in such a Europe a partner with whom we can deal on a basis of full equality in all the great and burdensome tasks of building and defending a community of free nations.

It would be premature at this time to do more than indicate the high regard with which we view the formation of this partnership. The first order of business is for our European friends to go forward in forming the more perfect union which will someday make this partnership possible.

A great new edifice is not built overnight. It was 11 years from the Declaration of Independence to the writing of the Constitution. The construction of workable federal institutions required still another generation. The greatest works of our Nation's founders lay not in documents and in declarations, but in creative, determined action. The building of the new house of Europe has followed the same practical, purposeful course. Building the Atlantic partnership now will not be easily or cheaply finished.

But I will say here and now, on this Day of Independence, that the United States will be ready for a Declaration of Interdependence, that we will be prepared to discuss with a united Europe the ways and means of forming a concrete Atlantic partnership, a mutually beneficial partnership between the new union now emerging in Europe and the old American Union founded here 175 years ago.

All this will not be completed in a year, but let the world know it is our goal.

In urging the adoption of the United States Constitution, Alexander Hamilton told his fellow New Yorkers 'to think continentally.' Today Americans must learn to think intercontinentally. ...

From John F. Kennedy, Presidential Library and Museum:
http://www.cs.umb.edu/jfklibrary/jfk-independencehall-1962.html

DOCUMENT 28   NIXON OUTLINING NEW ECONOMIC POLICY, 15 AUGUST 1971

As the European Community became increasingly competitive and as it was about to enlarge its membership, President Nixon recognised the competition and called for a readjustment in the economic and military relationship.

At the end of World War II the economies of the major industrial nations of Europe and Asia were shattered. To help them get on their feet and to protect their freedom, the United States has provided over the past 25 years $143 billion in foreign aid. That was the right thing for us to do.

Today, largely with our help, they have regained their vitality. They have become our strong competitors, and we welcome their success. But now that other nations are economically strong, the time has come for them to bear their share of the burden of defending freedom around the world. The time has come for exchange rates to be set straight and for the major nations to compete as equals. There is no longer any need for the United States to compete with one hand tied behind her back.

From Public Papers, The Richard Nixon Library and Birthplace:
http://www.nixonfoundation.org/Research_Center/1971_pdf_files/1971_0264.pdf

DOCUMENT 29   NIXON'S STATEMENT ON US COOPERATION WITH THE EUROPEAN ECONOMIC COMMUNITY, 27 OCTOBER 1972

This and the following document demonstrates some of the US ambivalence as the European Community began to enlarge its membership. US support is tempered with ongoing concerns about European competition.

I have read with great interest the communiqué issued by the leaders of the nine countries of the enlarged European Community, demonstrating once again their commitment to greater European unity. At this important meeting, the members of the Community have an objective of 'transforming the whole complex of their relations into a European Union by the end of the present decade.' The United States strongly supports that objective. It is, and has always been, my own deeply held view that progress toward a unified Europe enhances world peace, security and prosperity. ...

On behalf of the United States, I wish to reaffirm our commitment to work with the members of the European Community for reform of the international economic system in a way which will bring about a new freedom of world trade, new equity in international economic conduct, and effective solutions to the problems of the developing world. ...

From Public Papers, The Richard Nixon Library and Birthplace:
http://www.nixonfoundation.org/Research_Center/1972_pdf_files/1972_0378.pdf

DOCUMENT 30 NIXON'S REMARKS ON THE 'YEAR OF EUROPE', 15 FEBRUARY 1973

I have said this is the year of Europe. ... But the year of Europe becomes very important in both the economic context, which was brought home by the recent monetary situation, and also in terms of the national security context, because of the fact that MBFR – mutual balanced force reductions – will be a subject on our agenda this year.

... [Security and economic relations] were a major subject of discussion with Prime Minister Heath. Naturally, you would expect that these would lead to economic considerations – the problem of trade, which can be very interesting and sometimes very difficult – with our European friends as well as the Japanese ... .

From Public Papers, The Richard Nixon Library and Birthplace:
http://www.nixonfoundation.org/Research_Center/1973_pdf_files/1973_0045.pdf

DOCUMENT 31 THE OTTAWA DECLARATION ON ATLANTIC RELATIONS, 26 JUNE 1974

Signed by the membership of NATO, the Declaration reaffirmed the principles of the Atlantic Alliance. The text below and in documents 35 and 36 provide abbreviated extracts. The full texts are available on the NATO website.

1. The members of the North Atlantic Alliance declare that the treaty signed 25 years ago to protect their freedom and independence has confirmed their common destiny. Under the shield of the Treaty, the Allies have maintained their security, permitting them to preserve the values which are the heritage of their civilization and enabling Western Europe to rebuild from its ruins and lay the foundations of its unity.

2. The members of the Alliance reaffirm their conviction that the North Atlantic Treaty provides the indispensable basis for their security, thus making possible the pursuit of détente. They welcome the progress that has been achieved on the road towards détente and harmony among nations, and the fact that a Conference of 35 countries of Europe and North America is now seeking to lay down guidelines designed to increase security and cooperation in Europe. They believe that until circumstances permit the introduction of general, complete and controlled disarmament, which alone could provide genuine security for all, the ties uniting them must be maintained. The Allies share a common desire to reduce the burden of arms expenditure on their peoples. But States that wish to preserve peace have never achieved this aim by neglecting their own security.

DOCUMENT 33   THE TRANSATLANTIC DECLARATION, 1990

At the end of the Cold War and the impending demise of the Soviet Union, the prospects of a Europe undivided and democratic was both a cause for celebration and a particular concern for Washington. It worried that the Transatlantic ties might not remain as strong in the absence of a common defence purpose.

The United States of America on one side and, on the other, the European Community and its Member States, mindful of their common heritage and of their close historical, political, economic and cultural ties, guided by their faith in the values of human dignity, intellectual freedom and civil liberties, and in the democratic institutions which have evolved on both sides of the Atlantic over the centuries, recognizing that the transatlantic solidarity has been essential for the preservation of peace and freedom and for the development of free and prosperous economies as well as for the recent developments which have restored unity in Europe, determined to help consolidate the new Europe, undivided and democratic, resolved to strengthen security, economic cooperation and human rights in Europe in the framework of the CSCE, and in other fora, noting the firm commitment of the United States and the EC Member States concerned to the North Atlantic Alliance and to its principles and purposes, acting on the basis of a pattern of cooperation proven over many decades, and convinced that by strengthening and expanding this partnership on an equal footing they will greatly contribute to continued stability, as well as to political and economic progress in Europe and in the world, ... bearing in mind the accelerating process by which the European Community is acquiring its own identity in economic and monetary matters, in foreign policy and in the domain of security, determined further to strengthen transatlantic solidarity, through the variety of their international relations, have decided to endow their relationship with long-term perspectives.

Common Goals: The United States of America and the European Community and its Member States solemnly reaffirm their determination further to strengthen their partnership in order to: support democracy, the rule of law and respect for human rights and individual liberty, and promote prosperity and social progress world-wide; safeguard peace and promote international security, by cooperating with other nations against aggression and coercion, by contributing to the settlement of conflicts in the world and by reinforcing the role of the United Nations and other international organizations; pursue policies aimed at achieving a sound world economy marked by sustained economic growth with low inflation, a high level of employment, equitable social conditions, in a framework of international stability; promote market principles, reject protectionism and expand, strengthen and further open the multilateral trading system ... .

From Europa: The European Union Online: http://europa.eu.int/en/agenda/
eu-us/pub/decl.html

DOCUMENT 34   THE TREATY ON EUROPEAN UNION, 12 FEBRUARY 1992

The Treaty on the European Union signed in Maastricht accelerated European integration and increasingly extended it to include more political issues. Particularly of concern to the United States was the call for enhanced European independence and the move towards a common defence policy.

Resolved to mark a new stage in the process of European integration undertaken with the establishment of the European Communities; Recalling the historic importance of the ending of the division of the European continent and the need to create firm bases for the construction of the future Europe; Confirming their attachment to the principles of liberty, democracy and respect for human rights and fundamental freedoms and of the rule of law; Desiring to deepen the solidarity between their peoples while respecting their history, their culture and their traditions; Desiring to enhance further the democratic and efficient functioning of the institutions so as to enable them better to carry out, within a single institutional framework, the tasks entrusted to them; Resolved to achieve the strengthening and the convergence of their economies and to establish an economic and monetary union including, in accordance with the provisions of this Treaty, a single and stable currency; Determined to promote economic and social progress for their peoples, within the context of the accomplishment of the internal market and of reinforced cohesion and environmental protection, and to implement policies ensuring that advances in economic integration are accompanied by parallel progress in other fields; Resolved to establish a citizenship common to the nationals of their countries; Resolved to implement a common foreign and security policy including the eventual framing of a common defence policy, which might in time lead to a common defence, thereby reinforcing the European identity and its independence in order to promote peace, security and progress in Europe and in the world; Reaffirming their objective to facilitate the free movement of persons while ensuring the safety and security of their peoples, by including provisions on justice and home affairs in this Treaty; Resolved to continue the process of creating an ever closer union among the peoples of Europe, in which decisions are taken as closely as possible to the citizen in price of oil, leading to crisis in the West. US support for Israel in the 1973 Arab–Israeli War led to a total embargo of oil from OPEC. The EC faced much more limited restrictions, except for the Netherlands.

Ostpolitik   was conceived in West Germany as an attempt to improve relations with the Soviet Union and Eastern Europe from 1966 onwards. The process accelerated after Willy Brandt became Chancellor in 1969. The process led to several agreements with the Soviets, East Europe and East Germany. *Ostpolitik* provided Germany with greater independence from US policies. It was a European forerunner to the superpower *détente*.

Perestroika   was introduced as a programme for restructuring the Soviet Union from 1986 by Mikhail Gorbachev. The concept symbolised the drastic need for Soviet reform in the late 1980s.

Prague Spring   refers to the attempt at liberalisation in Czechoslovakia during the spring of 1968. The process was brought to an end in August with a Warsaw Pact intervention.

'Seven, the'   see European Free Trade Association.

'Six, the'   see European Economic Community.

Solidarity   was the trade union movement that organised widespread strikes across Poland in 1980 and 1981. Led by Lech Walesa, the movement agitated against the economic conditions of the period. With the build-up of Soviet troops on the borders of Poland, General Jaruzelski imposed martial law in 1981. Walesa was released from prison and continued semi-covert resistance throughout the decade. He was elected President of Poland in 1990.

Strategic Arms Limitation Talks (SALT) I and II   SALT I was signed in May 1972 during *détente* in an attempt to place a limit on both superpower's intercontinental ballistic missiles. The agreement included the Anti-Ballistic Missile (ABM) Treaty, which limited the development of protective missile systems. The ABM treaty ran into trouble with both Reagan's proposal to initiate SDI and Bush's proposal to initiate NMD. SALT II was agreed in June 1979. It imposed an upper limit on the various strategic arms both superpowers could possess.

Strategic Defense Initiative (SDI)   or 'Star Wars' was initiated in 1983 by the Reagan administration. It envisaged a space-based missile defence system that could intercept Soviet intercontinental missiles. Though funding for the project was lavish, it was largely believed to be untenable by scientific commentators. It proved to be the sticking block in the superpower negotiations during the late 1980s.

Versailles Treaty   was signed between Germany and the Allies following the First World War in 1919. Germany accepted arms limitations, the loss of territory in Europe and its colonial areas and, crucially, the 'war guilt' clause, which became a part of the basis of Hitler's grievances during the 1920s.

Warsaw Pact   was created as a military alliance of East European states with the Soviet Union as a response to West German rearmament in 1955. The Pact initially included the Soviet Union, Albania, Romania, Poland, Hungary, Czechoslovakia, Bulgaria, and East Germany. Its principal military actions were taken against member states: Hungary in 1956 and Czechoslovakia in 1968.

Young Plan   was arranged in 1929 to reduce and reschedule German reparation payments to the Allies.

Acheson, Dean (1893–1971) Influential US diplomat and Under-Secretary of State in the Roosevelt administration, particularly involved in Lend Lease and Bretton Woods. In the Truman administration he eventually served as Secretary of State from 1949 to 1953. He was a key proponent of containment and advocate of NATO.

Adams, John Quincy (1767–1848) US Secretary of State between 1817 and 1825, he was the architect of the Monroe Doctrine, which in part was motivated by his severe dislike of the British. He served one term as President from 1825 to 1829.

Adenauer, Konrad (1876–1967) Chancellor to the Federal Republic of Germany from its inception in 1949 to 1963. Adenauer was Chairman of the Christian Democratic Union until 1966. He refused to recognise East Germany throughout his tenure and formed extensive links with the West. He took West Germany into the ECSC, NATO and the EEC. Politically he was close to de Gaulle, creating a Franco–German alliance in Europe.

Andropov, Yuri (1914–84) Soviet Ambassador to Hungary during the 1956 uprising and later Head of the KGB. In 1982 he became General Secretary of the Communist Party. As such he advanced further *détente* and specific non-aggression pacts with the United States, which were rejected. He was an early sponsor of Gorbachev.

Attlee, Clement (1883–1967) Attlee was a member of the coalition cabinet during the Second World War under Churchill. He was the leader of the British Labour Party from 1935 and served as Prime Minister from 1945 to 1951. He was the British representative for the second half of the Potsdam Conference and later tried to initiate US–Soviet cooperation.

Beneš, Eduard (1884–1948) Beneš, head of the National Socialist Party, presided over a coalition government in Czechoslovakia from 1945 to 1948 as President. Communist pressure precluded participation in the Marshall Plan. In February 1948 the Communists seized total power.

Bevin, Ernest (1881–1951) British Foreign Secretary during the Attlee government until his resignation in 1951 on health grounds. He opposed Attlee's stance on the Soviet Union and became a key power behind the Brussels Treaty and British entry into NATO. He recognised that Europe offered some respite from US influence and was a key figure in the OEEC.

Bidault, Georges (1899–1983) Served as French Foreign Minister under de Gaulle from 1944. Though oriented towards the West and a key figure in both the OEEC and NATO, his principal concern was German revival. As such he was courted by the Soviet Union.

Brandt, Willy (1913–92)   Mayor of West Berlin during the 1961 crisis Brandt rose to prominence. In 1967 he joined a coalition of parties and in 1969 he became Chancellor of West Germany. He was principally concerned with advancing *Ostpolitik*, extending relations with the Soviet bloc, which presaged the period of *détente*.

Brezhnev, Leonid (1906–82)   Soviet General Secretary of the Communist Party from 1964 to 1982. Brezhnev built up Soviet nuclear forces to equal those of the US. In 1968 he presided over the Soviet invasion of Czechoslovakia and formulated the Brezhnev Doctrine. The poor state of the Soviet economy necessitated engagement with Germany's *Ostpolitik* and US *détente*.

Briand, Aristide (1862–1932)   Represented France as the premier at the Washington Conference. By 1925 he became Foreign Minister and was instrumental in arranging the Locarno Treaty with Germany and, ultimately, was a co-creator of the multilateral treaty bearing his name.

Bryan, William Jennings (1860–1925)   An anti-imperialist in the United States during the late nineteenth century. He served as Woodrow Wilson's Secretary of State between 1913 and 1915. He eventually resigned over the US insistence of neutrality rights during the First World War.

Bush, George (1924–)   Bush acted as US representative to the UN and as head of the CIA during the 1970s. In the 1980s he was Vice President during the Reagan administration; he served as President from 1989 to 1993. He presided over the end of the Cold War and German unification in 1990, though his cautious approach to European issues diminished US influence.

Caetano, Marcelo (1906–80)   Minister in the Portuguese Salazar regime. He succeeded Salazar in 1966 and served as Prime Minister till 1974. His inability to deal with Portuguese colonial issues in Mozambique and Angola lead to the Carnation Revolution which ousted him from power.

Carter, Jimmy (1924–)   US President from 1977 to 1981, Carter did not engage with European affairs that extensively. His foreign policy emphasised human rights and he successfully negotiated the SALT II treaties with the Soviet Union in 1977.

Ceauçescu, Nikolai (1918–89)   General Secretary of the Romanian Communist Party from 1965 and Head of State from 1967. He withdrew Romania from the Warsaw Pact and condemned the Soviet invasion of Czechoslovakia in 1968. During *détente* he increased his ties to the West. Resisting demands for reform, he was eventually executed in December 1989.

Chamberlain, Neville (1869–1940)   British Prime Minister from 1937 to 1940. He was criticised extensively for the policy of appeasement of Nazi Germany and Italy, in which a portion of Czechoslovakia was handed to Germany in exchange for 'peace in our time'. He was succeeded by Winston Churchill.

Chernenko, Konstantin (1911–85)   Soviet General Secretary from 1984 to 1985. Chernenko was incapacitated by ill health for most of his period in power. His conservative approach to Soviet foreign policies brought no new initiatives.

Churchill, Winston (1874–1965)   Twice British Prime Minister from 1940 to 1945 and 1951 to 1955, Churchill was instrumental in engaging Roosevelt and US power in the Second World War and yet resisting pressure to decolonise the British Empire. His famous 'Iron Curtain' speech defined the early Cold War period, though he later advocated superpower summitry during the 1950s.

Coolidge, Calvin (1872–1933)   Vice President under the Harding administration, Coolidge became US President in 1923 and served till 1929. Though the United States pursued limited political isolation, its economy was expanding and engaged in European affairs. Under Coolidge the Dawes and Young Plans were negotiated to alleviate the question of German reparations.

De Gaulle, Charles (1890–1970)   Leader of the Free French during the Second World War he resigned in 1946. His return to politics in 1958 placed him in a key position in European politics. He enhanced relations with the Adenauer government in Germany and together formed the backbone of the original 'Six' of the EEC. During the 1960s he twice vetoed British entry to the EEC, fearing US influence, and subsequently withdrew French forces from the NATO command structure in 1966.

Dubček, Alexander (1921–92)   First Secretary of the Czechoslovakian Communist Party from January 1968, he quickly initiated a period of liberalisation and reform known as the Prague Spring. The Soviet Union invaded in August 1968 to halt the direction and speed of the changes. Dubček briefly returned to politics in 1989 after the Czech revolution.

Dulles, John Foster (1888–1959)   US Secretary of State from 1953 to 1959. He was a fierce critic of the Soviet Union and communism and advocated 'rolling back' communist power in Eastern Europe. His tough stance on communism enhanced the Atlantic Alliance and NATO, but he was also instrumental in US opposition to the British and French action in Suez.

Eden, Anthony (1897–1977)   Eden resigned as British Foreign Secretary in 1938 after Chamberlain's appeasement of Germany, but returned to the cabinet during the Second World War. Eden became Prime Minister in 1955 (following Churchill) till 1957. He was instrumental in gaining acceptance for German rearmament and entry into NATO in 1955. His actions at Suez, however, antagonised the US and he resigned shortly after.

Eisenhower, Dwight (1890–1969)   Eisenhower was Supreme Allied Commander in the European theatre during the Second World War and later, in 1950, was appointed head of NATO. An initially vociferous opponent of the Soviet Union, his approach was more cautious. His administration opposed British and French action at Suez in 1956 and failed to intervene in the Hungarian Revolution which was encouraged by the US.

Erhard, Ludwig (1897–1977)   German Chancellor from 1963 to 1966. He was the architect of the German economic recovery from 1949 onwards. In 1963 his policies moved him away from the close relations that de Gaulle had with Adenauer, to a more pro-US inclination. He nevertheless initiated further contact with the East European governments.

Franco, Francisco (1892–1975)   Leader of the nationalist forces during the Spanish Civil War, Franco's authoritarian rule of Spain lasted till 1975.

Concentration on economic aspects of US diplomacy increased since the late 1950s with the influence of the revisionists. For an influential overview of US diplomacy, see William Appleman Williams (1959) *The Tragedy of American Diplomacy* (New York: Delta). Lloyd Gardner's (1964) *Economic Aspects of New Deal Diplomacy* (Madison, WI: University of Wisconsin Press) is an extremely detailed analysis of the Roosevelt period. Covering the Cold War in general, see Thomas McCormick's (1989) *America's Half Century: United States Foreign Policy in the Cold War* (Baltimore, MD: Johns Hopkins Press). Works on the economic relations with varying perspectives include William H. Becker and Samuel F. Wells (eds) (1984) *Economics and World Power: An Assessment of American Diplomacy since 1789* (New York: Columbia University Press); Diane Kunz (1997) *Butter and Guns: America's Cold War Economic Diplomacy* (New York: The Free Press); David Calleo's (1982) *The Imperious Economy* (Cambridge, MA: Harvard University Press); Paul Kennedy's (1989) *The Rise and Fall of Great Powers: Economic Change and Military Conflict from 1500 to 2000* (London: Fontana) and Norman Levine's (ed.) (1996) *The US and the EU: Economic Relations in a World of Transition* (Reading, MA: University Press of America). Noted works that cover more particular periods or relationships are Alan Milward's (1984) *The Reconstruction of Western Europe 1945–51* (Berkeley: University of California Press); Michael Hogan's (1987) *The Marshall Plan* (Cambridge: Cambridge University Press); Thomas Zeiler's (1992) *American Trade and Power in the 1960s* on economic issues; Alan Dobson's (1988) *The Politics of the Anglo-American Economic Special Relationship, 1940–1987* (Brighton: Wheatsheaf Books) and Ian Jackson's (2001) *The Economic Cold War: America, Britain and East–West Trade, 1948–63* (London: Palgrave).

The ideological foundations of US foreign policy can be found in Michael Hunt (1987) *Ideology and US Foreign Policy* (New Haven, CT: Yale University Press) and constructions of the ideas that informed US policy in David Ryan (2000) *US Foreign Policy in World History* (London: Routledge). Tony Smith (1994) *America's Mission: The United States and the Worldwide Struggle for Democracy in the Twentieth Century* (Princeton, NJ: Princeton University Press) provides a detailed analysis of the influence of Wilson on US diplomacy, as does Frank Ninkovich's (2001) *The Wilsonian Century: US Foreign Policy since 1900* (Chicago: University of Chicago Press).

Work covering the Wilsonian period is voluminous. For early interpretations, see Charles Tansill (1938) *America Goes to War* (Boston: Little Brown Company) and George Kennan's (1951) *American Diplomacy, 1900–1950* (Chicago: Chicago University Press). Robert Osgood (1953) *Ideals and Self-Interest in America's Foreign Relations: The Great Transformation of the Twentieth Century* (Chicago: University of Chicago Press) was an early standard text on Wilsonian diplomacy, as was the multi-volume work by Arthur Link (1960–65) *Wilson* (Princeton, NJ: Princeton Univerity Press), in which the idea of 'higher realism' is put forth. Lloyd Ambrosius (1987) *Woodrow Wilson and the American Diplomatic Tradition* (Cambridge: Cambridge University Press) was particularly influential, as was Lloyd Gardner's (1984) *Safe for Democracy: The Anglo-American Response to Revolution, 1913–1923* (New York: Oxford University Press) which looks at Anglo-American reactions to nationalism. More recently, Thomas Knock (1992) *To End All Wars: Woodrow Wilson and the Quest for a New World Order* (Oxford: Oxford University Press) examines Wilson's struggle to create a new world order.

On the inter-war period, see Robert A. Divine (1962) *The Illusion of Neutrality* (Chicago: University of Chicago Press) and Robert H. Ferrell (1957) *American Diplomacy in the Great Depression: Hoover–Stimson Foreign Policy, 1929–1933* (New York: Norton), both of which examine the traditional approach to the period of US 'isolationism'. After Wilson's ambitious agenda for engagement, these works chart the more limited scope of the Republican administrations through the 1920s and early 1930s. By the late 1950s revisionist accounts became prominent, arguing that the United States had always been expansionist since its independence and that during the 1920s and 1930s it remained so, though the emphasis was on economic and cultural engagement. See for instance: William Appleman Williams (1959) *The Tragedy of American Diplomacy* and Lloyd C. Gardner's (1964) *Economic Aspects of New Deal Diplomacy*. An interpretation giving primary importance to the role of corporations ('corporatism') is provided by Michael J. Hogan (1977) *Informal Entente: The Private Structure of Cooperation in Anglo-American Economic Diplomacy, 1918–1929* (Missouri), and Joan Hoff Wilson's (1971) *American Business and Foreign Policy, 1920–1933* (New York: Houghton Mifflin). US cultural expansion during the period is covered by Emily S. Rosenberg (1982) *Spreading the American Dream: American Economic and Cultural Expansion 1890–1945* (New York: Hill and Wang) and by Frank Costigliola's (1984) *Awkward Dominion: America's Political, Economic, and Cultural Relations with Europe, 1919–1933* (Ithaca, NY: Cornell University Press). Akira Iriye's (1993) *The Globalizing of America, 1913–1945* (Cambridge: Cambridge University Press) provides a good synthesis that also emphasises issues of culture. Brian McKercher (1999) treats the erosion of British hegemony and the rise of US power in *Transition of Power: Britain's Loss of Global Pre-Eminence to the United States 1930–1945* (Cambridge: Cambridge University Press).

The literature on the war is extensive. Start with Warren Kimball's (1991) *The Juggler: Franklin Roosevelt as Wartime Statesman* (Princeton, NJ: Princeton University Press). Robert Dallek (1979) *Franklin D. Roosevelt and American Foreign Policy 1932–1945* (Oxford: Oxford University Press) and Robert Divine (1968) *The Reluctant Belligerent: American Entry into World War II* (New York: Wiley) examines US entry into the war. Gabriel Kolko's (1970) *The Politics of War: The World and United States Foreign Policy 1943–1945* (New York: Random House) provides a revisionist critique. A good review of the literature on the war can be found in Mark Stoler's essay 'A Half Century of Conflict' in Michael J. Hogan's (1995) *America and the World: The Historiography of American Foreign Relations since 1941* (Cambridge: Cambridge University Press). See also Martin Gilbert's (1981) *Auschwitz and the Allies* (New York: Henry Holt).

The origins of the Cold War has generated an inordinate amount of controversy and historiographical dispute. See Louis Halle (1963) *The Cold War as History* (New York: Harper & Row) for an early statement of a traditional interpretation. Revisionists challenged the traditional interpretations from the late 1950s onward. See, for example, Joyce and Gabriel Kolko's (1972) *The Limits of Power: The World and the United States Foreign Policy, 1945–1954* (New York: Harper & Row) and, covering the entire post-war period Walter LaFeber's perennial *America, Russia, and the Cold War* (New York: McGraw-Hill, 1991, 1993, 1997). Post-revisionists began to influence the field from the early 1970s. See especially John Lewis Gaddis (1972) *The United States and the Origins of the Cold War* (New York: Columbia University

Press) and his (1982) *Strategies of Containment* (Oxford: Oxford University Press) which is a very good post-revisionist argument. Gaddis's (1997) *We Now Know: Rethinking Cold War History* (Oxford: Clarendon Press) provides a vindication of US policy for the origins of the Cold War. A very good analysis of the issues and the literature is David Reynolds (ed.) (1994) *The Origins of the Cold War in Europe: International Perspectives* (New Haven, CT: Yale University Press). More recent influential books include Melvyn Leffler's (1992) *A Preponderance of Power: National Security, the Truman Administration, and the Cold War* (Stanford, CA: Stanford University Press) and Michael Hogan's (1998) *Cross of Iron: Harry S. Truman and the Origins of the National Security State, 1945–1954* (Cambridge: Cambridge University Press).

The literature on the end of the Cold War is growing rapidly. A work of huge detail is Raymond Garthoff's (1994) *The Great Transition: American–Soviet Relations and the End of the Cold War* (Washington, DC: The Brookings Institution). His earlier work is also tremendously influential, see Garthoff (1994) *Détente and Confrontation: American–Soviet Relations from Nixon to Reagan* (Washington, DC: The Brookings Institution). Michael Hogan's (1992) edited collection, *The End of the Cold War: Its Meaning and Implications* (Cambridge: Cambridge University Press) provides a useful introduction because of the range of opinion contained in the volume. Another work of interest includes Michael Beschloss and Strobe Talbott's (1993) *At the Highest Levels: The Inside Story of the End of the Cold War* (London: Warner). David Calleo's (1987) *Beyond American Hegemony: The Future of the Western Alliance* (New York: Basic Books) looks at the Alliance up to the easing of tensions between the superpowers. John Lewis Gaddis (1992) *The United States and the End of the Cold War* (Oxford: Oxford University Press) provides a good collection of essays. Of particular note are three books that exclusively examine the transatlantic relationship: Kevin Featherstone and Roy Ginsberg's (1996) *The United States and the European Community in the 1990s: Partners in Transition* (New York: St Martin's Press); John Peterson (1993) *Europe and America: The Prospects for Partnership* (New York: Routledge), which examines the prospects for the continued Alliance; and René Schwok (1991) *US–EC Relations in the Post-Cold War Era: Conflict or Partnership* (Boulder, CO: Westview Press), which examines the theme of conflict and cooperation in the relationship.

Particular bilateral relationships to note are David Dimbleby and David Reynolds (1988) *An Ocean Apart: The Relationship between Britain and America in the Twentieth Century* (London: Hodder and Stoughton), which provides a concise overview of Anglo-American relations. Alan Dobson's (1995) *Anglo-American Relations in the Twentieth Century: Of Friendship, Conflict and the Rise and Decline of Superpowers* (London: Routledge) examines the transition from one power to the next and the conflict and cooperation that ensued. John Dumbrell's (2001) *A Special Relationship: Anglo-American Relations in the Cold War and After* (London: Macmillan) is very useful for its focus on the post-1960s period and the tensions that developed over Vietnam and Ireland. William R. Louis and Hedley Bull (eds) (1986) *The Special Relationship: Anglo-American Relations since 1945* (Oxford: Clarendon Press) provides a very useful collection of essays. On France, see Frank Costigliola (1992) *France and the United States: The Cold War Alliance since World War II* (New York: Twayne Publishing); Robert Paxton and Nicholas Wahl (eds) (1994) *De Gaulle and the United States: A Centenial Reappraisal* (Oxford:

Berg); Jean-Baptiste Duroselle (1978) *France and the United States from the Beginnings to the Present* (Chicago: University of Chicago Press); Irwin Wall (1991) *The United States and the Making of Postwar France, 1945–1954* (Cambridge: Cambridge University Press); and Philip Gordon (1995) *France, Germany and the Western Alliance* (Boulder, CO: Westview Press). On Germany, see Manfred Jonas (1984) *The United States and Germany: A Diplomatic History* (Ithaca, NY: Cornell University Press); Frank Ninkovich (1995) *Germany and the United States: The Transformation of the German Question since 1945* (New York: Twayne Publishing); Thomas Schwartz (1991) *America's Germany: John J. McCloy and the Federal Republic of Germany* (Cambridge, MA: Harvard University Press); and Frank Mayer (1996) *Adenauer and Kennedy: A Study in German-American Relations, 1961–1963* (New York: St Martin's Press).

Powaski, Ronald E. (1987) *March to Armageddon: The United States and the Nuclear Arms Race, 1939 to the Present*. New York: Oxford University Press.

Prados, John (1986) *Presidents' Secret Wars: CIA and Pentagon Covert Operations from World War II through Iranscam*. New York: William Morrow.

Reynolds, David (1992) 'Beyond Bipolarity in Space and Time', in Michael J. Hogan (ed.), *The End of the Cold War: Its Meaning and Implications*. Cambridge: Cambridge University Press.

Reynolds, David (2000) *One World Divisible: A Global History since 1945*. London: Penguin.

Roberts, J. M. (1996) *A History of Europe*. Oxford: Helicon Publishing.

Rosenberg, Emily S. (1982) *Spreading the American Dream: American Economic and Cultural Expansion, 1890–1945*. New York: Hill and Wang.

Rupieper, Hermann-Josef (1992) 'After the Cold War: The United States, Germany, and European Security', in Michael J. Hogan (ed.), *End of the Cold War*. Cambridge: Cambridge University Press.

Ryan, David (1995) 'Asserting US Power', in John Philip Davies (ed.), *American Quarter Century*. Manchester: Manchester University Press.

Ryan, David (2000) *US Foreign Policy in World History*. London: Routledge.

Ryan, David and Victor Pungong (eds) (2000) *The United States and Decolonization: Power and Freedom*. London: Macmillan.

Sandle, Mark (1997) *A Short History of Soviet Socialism*. London: UCL.

Schulzinger, Robert D. (1990) *American Diplomacy in the Twentieth Century*. New York: Oxford University Press.

Schwartz, Thomas A. (1994) 'Victories and Defeats in the Long Twilight Struggle: The United States and Western Europe in the 1960s', in Diane B. Kunz (ed.), *The Diplomacy of the Crucial Decade: American Foreign Relations during the 1960s*. New York: Columbia University Press.

Shaw, Albert (1924) *The Messages and Papers of Woodrow Wilson* (Vol. 1). New York: The Review of Reviews Corporation.

Sherry, Michael S. (1995) *In the Shadow of War: The United States since the 1930s*. New Haven, CT: Yale University Press.

Smith, Gaddis (1994) *The Last Years of the Monroe Doctrine, 1945–1993*. New York: Hill and Wang.

Smith, Tony (1994) *America's Mission: The United States and the Worldwide Struggle for Democracy in the Twentieth Century*. Princeton, NJ: Princeton University Press.

Stephanson, Anders (1995) *Manifest Destiny: American Expansion and the Empire of Right*. New York: Hill and Wang.

Storeheier, Heidi (1996) 'US Policy Towards the European Free Trade Association 1959–1963', Department of History, Norwegian University of Technology and Science.

Talbott, Strobe (1999) Talbott on Euro-Atlantic Community and Nato Summit at the German Society for Foreign Policy. United States Information Service, 5 February.

Thorne, Christopher (1978) *Allies of a Kind: The United States, Britain, and the War against Japan*. New York: Oxford University Press.

Tuchman, Barbara (1958) *The Zimmerman Telegram: How the United States Entered the Great War*. London: Macmillan.

Tucker, Robert W. and David C. Hendrickson (1993) 'America and Bosnia', *The National Interest* 33 (Fall).

Walker, Martin (1993) *The Cold War and the Making of the Modern World*. London: Fourth Estate.

Wegs, J. Robert (1984) *Europe since 1945: A Concise History*. New York: St Martin's Press.

Williams, William Appleman (1959) *The Tragedy of American Diplomacy*. New York: Delta.

Williams, William Appleman, Thomas McCormick, Lloyd Gardner and Walter LaFeber (eds) (1989) *America in Vietnam: A Documentary History*. New York: W. W. Norton.

Wilson, Kevin and Jan van der Dussen (eds) (1993) *The History of the Idea of Europe*. London: Routledge.

Winand, Pascaline (1993) *Eisenhower, Kennedy, and the United States of Europe*. New York: St Martin's Press.

Wood, Robert E. (1994) 'From the Marshall Plan to the Third World', in Melvyn P. Leffler and David S. Painter (eds), *Origins of the Cold War: An International History*. London: Routledge.

Yergin, Daniel (1991) *The Prize: The Epic Quest for Oil, Money and Power*. London: Simon and Schuster.

Young, John W. (1993) *Britain and European Unity, 1945–1992*. London: Macmillan.

Zinn, Howard (1980) *A People's History of the United States*. London: Longman.

INDEX

SEMINAR STUDIES IN HISTORY

General Editors: Clive Emsley & Gordon Martel

The series was founded by Patrick Richardson in 1966. Between 1980 and 1996 Roger Lockyer edited the series before handing over to Clive Emsley (Professor of History at the Open University) and Gordon Martel (Professor of International History at the University of Northern British Columbia, Canada and Senior Research Fellow at De Montfort University).

MEDIEVAL ENGLAND

The Pre-Reformation Church in England 1400–1530 (Second edition)
Christopher Harper-Bill   0 582 28989 0

Lancastrians and Yorkists: The Wars of the Roses
David R Cook   0 582 35384 X

Family and Kinship in England 1450–1800
Will Coster   0 582 35717 9

TUDOR ENGLAND

Henry VII (Third edition)
Roger Lockyer & Andrew Thrush   0 582 20912 9

Henry VIII (Second edition)
M D Palmer   0 582 35437 4

Tudor Rebellions (Fourth edition)
Anthony Fletcher & Diarmaid MacCulloch   0 582 28990 4

The Reign of Mary I (Second edition)
Robert Tittler   0 582 06107 5

Early Tudor Parliaments 1485–1558
Michael A R Graves   0 582 03497 3

The English Reformation 1530–1570
W J Sheils   0 582 35398 X

Elizabethan Parliaments 1559–1601 (Second edition)
Michael A R Graves   0 582 29196 8

England and Europe 1485–1603 (Second edition)
Susan Doran   0 582 28991 2

The Church of England 1570–1640
Andrew Foster   0 582 35574 5

STUART BRITAIN

Social Change and Continuity: England 1550–1750 (Second edition)
Barry Coward   0 582 29442 8

James I (Second edition)
S J Houston   0 582 20911 0

The English Civil War 1640–1649
Martyn Bennett   0 582 35392 0

Charles I, 1625–1640
Brian Quintrell   0 582 00354 7

The English Republic 1649–1660 (Second edition)
Toby Barnard   0 582 08003 7

Radical Puritans in England 1550–1660
R J Acheson   0 582 35515 X

The Restoration and the England of Charles II (Second edition)
John Miller   0 582 29223 9

The Glorious Revolution (Second edition)
John Miller   0 582 29222 0

EARLY MODERN EUROPE

The Renaissance (Second edition)
Alison Brown   0 582 30781 3

The Emperor Charles V
Martyn Rady   0 582 35475 7

French Renaissance Monarchy: Francis I and Henry II (Second edition)
Robert Knecht   0 582 28707 3

The Protestant Reformation in Europe
Andrew Johnston   0 582 07020 1

The French Wars of Religion 1559–1598 (Second edition)
Robert Knecht   0 582 28533 X

Phillip II
Geoffrey Woodward   0 582 07232 8

The Thirty Years' War
Peter Limm   0 582 35373 4

Louis XIV
Peter Campbell   0 582 01770 X

Spain in the Seventeenth Century
Graham Darby   0 582 07234 4

Peter the Great
William Marshall   0 582 00355 5

EUROPE 1789–1918

Britain and the French Revolution
Clive Emsley   0 582 36961 4

Revolution and Terror in France 1789–1795 (Second edition)
D G Wright   0 582 00379 2

Napoleon and Europe
D G Wright   0 582 35457 9

The Abolition of Serfdom in Russia, 1762–1907
David Moon   0 582 29486 X

Nineteenth-Century Russia: Opposition to Autocracy
Derek Offord   0 582 35767 5

The Constitutional Monarchy in France 1814–48
Pamela Pilbeam   0 582 31210 8

The 1848 Revolutions (Second edition)
Peter Jones   0 582 06106 7

The Italian Risorgimento
M Clark   0 582 00353 9

Bismarck & Germany 1862–1890 (Second edition)
D G Williamson   0 582 29321 9

Imperial Germany 1890–1918
Ian Porter, Ian Armour and Roger Lockyer   0 582 03496 5

The Dissolution of the Austro-Hungarian Empire 1867–1918 (Second edition)
John W Mason   0 582 29466 5

Second Empire and Commune: France 1848–1871 (Second edition)
William H C Smith   0 582 28705 7

France 1870–1914 (Second edition)
Robert Gildea   0 582 29221 2

The Scramble for Africa (Second edition)
M E Chamberlain   0 582 36881 2

Late Imperial Russia 1890–1917
John F Hutchinson   0 582 32721 0

The First World War
Stuart Robson   0 582 31556 5

Austria, Prussia and Germany, 1806–1871
John Breuilly   0 582 43739 3

EUROPE SINCE 1918

The Russian Revolution (Second edition)
Anthony Wood   0 582 35559 1

Lenin's Revolution: Russia, 1917–1921
David Marples   0 582 31917 X

Stalin and Stalinism (Third edition)
Martin McCauley   0 582 50587 9

The Weimar Republic (Second edition)
John Hiden   0 582 28706 5

The Inter-War Crisis 1919–1939
Richard Overy   0 582 35379 3

Fascism and the Right in Europe, 1919–1945
Martin Blinkhorn   0 582 07021 X

Spain's Civil War (Second edition)
Harry Browne   0 582 28988 2

The Third Reich (Third edition)
D G Williamson   0 582 20914 5

The Origins of the Second World War (Second edition)
R J Overy   0 582 29085 6

The Second World War in Europe
Paul MacKenzie   0 582 32692 3

The French at War, 1934–1944
Nicholas Atkin   0 582 36899 5

Anti-Semitism before the Holocaust
Albert S Lindemann   0 582 36964 9

The Holocaust: The Third Reich and the Jews
David Engel   0 582 32720 2

Germany from Defeat to Partition, 1945–1963
D G Williamson   0 582 29218 2

Britain and Europe since 1945
Alex May   0 582 30778 3

Eastern Europe 1945–1969: From Stalinism to Stagnation
Ben Fowkes   0 582 32693 1

Eastern Europe since 1970
Bülent Gökay   0 582 32858 6

The Khrushchev Era, 1953–1964
Martin McCauley   0 582 27776 0

Hitler and the Rise of the Nazi Party
Frank McDonough   0 582 50606 9

The Soviet Union Under Brezhnev
William Tompson   0 582 32719 9

NINETEENTH-CENTURY BRITAIN

Britain before the Reform Acts: Politics and Society 1815–1832
Eric J Evans   0 582 00265 6

Parliamentary Reform in Britain c. 1770–1918
Eric J Evans   0 582 29467 3

Democracy and Reform 1815–1885
D G Wright   0 582 31400 3

Poverty and Poor Law Reform in Nineteenth-Century Britain, 1834–1914:
From Chadwick to Booth
David Englander   0 582 31554 9

The Birth of Industrial Britain: Economic Change, 1750–1850
Kenneth Morgan   0 582 29833 4

Chartism (Third edition)
Edward Royle   0 582 29080 5

Peel and the Conservative Party 1830–1850
Paul Adelman   0 582 35557 5

Gladstone, Disraeli and later Victorian Politics (Third edition)
Paul Adelman   0 582 29322 7

Britain and Ireland: From Home Rule to Independence
Jeremy Smith   0 582 30193 9

TWENTIETH-CENTURY BRITAIN

The Rise of the Labour Party 1880–1945 (Third edition)
Paul Adelman   0 582 29210 7

The Conservative Party and British Politics 1902–1951
Stuart Ball   0 582 08002 9

The Decline of the Liberal Party 1910–1931 (Second edition)
Paul Adelman   0 582 27733 7

The British Women's Suffrage Campaign 1866–1928
Harold L Smith   0 582 29811 3

War & Society in Britain 1899–1948
Rex Pope   0 582 03531 7

The British Economy since 1914: A Study in Decline?
Rex Pope   0 582 30194 7

Unemployment in Britain between the Wars
Stephen Constantine   0 582 35232 0

The Attlee Governments 1945–1951
Kevin Jefferys   0 582 06105 9

The Conservative Governments 1951–1964
Andrew Boxer   0 582 20913 7

Britain under Thatcher
Anthony Seldon and Daniel Collings   0 582 31714 2

Britain and Empire, 1880–1945
Dane Kennedy   0 582 41493 8

INTERNATIONAL HISTORY

The Eastern Question 1774–1923 (Second edition)
A L Macfie   0 582 29195 X

India 1885–1947: The Unmaking of an Empire
Ian Copland   0 582 38173 8

The Origins of the First World War (Second edition)
Gordon Martel   0 582 28697 2

The United States and the First World War
Jennifer D Keene   0 582 35620 2

Women and the First World War
Susan R Grayzel   0 582 41876 3

Anti-Semitism before the Holocaust
Albert S Lindemann   0 582 36964 9

The Origins of the Cold War, 1941–1949 (Third edition)
Martin McCauley   0 582 77284 2

Russia, America and the Cold War, 1949–1991
Martin McCauley   0 582 27936 4

The Arab–Israeli Conflict
Kirsten E Schulze   0 582 31646 4

The United Nations since 1945: Peacekeeping and the Cold War
Norrie MacQueen   0 582 35673 3

Decolonisation: The British Experience since 1945
Nicholas J White   0 582 29087 2

WORLD HISTORY

China in Transformation 1900–1949
Colin Mackerras   0 582 31209 4

Japan Faces the World, 1925–1952
Mary L Hanneman   0 582 36898 7

Japan in Transformation, 1952–2000
Jeff Kingston   0 582 41875 5

China since 1949
Linda Benson   0 582 35722 5

US HISTORY

American Abolitionists
Stanley Harrold   0 582 35738 1

The American Civil War, 1861–1865
Reid Mitchell   0 582 31973 0

America in the Progressive Era, 1890–1914
Lewis L Gould   0 582 35671 7

The United States and the First World War
Jennifer D Keene   0 582 35620 2

The Truman Years, 1945–1953
Mark S Byrnes   0 582 32904 3

The Korean War
Steven Hugh Lee   0 582 31988 9

The Origins of the Vietnam War
Fredrik Logevall   0 582 31918 8

The Vietnam War
Mitchell Hall   0 582 32859 4

American Expansionism, 1783–1860
Mark S. Joy   0 582 36965 7

The United States and Europe in the Twentieth Century
David Ryan   0 582 30864 X

East Meets West in Dance

Voices in the Cross-Cultural Dialogue

KINGSTON COLLEGE

00116084

Choreography and Dance Studies

A series of books edited by Robert P. Cohan, C.B.E.

Please see the back of this book for other titles in the Choreography and Dance Studies series.